EYEWITNESS

to

CRUCIFIXION

"Worst torture of all"
—SENECA, ADVISOR TO EMPEROR NERO

EYEWITNESS

to

CRUCIFIXION

THE **ROMANS**, THE **CROSS**, AND THE **SACRIFICE OF JESUS**

STEPHEN M. MILLER

Our Daily Bread
Publishing™

Interior design by Sherri L. Hoffman

Library of Congress Cataloging-in-Publication Data

Names: Miller, Stephen M., 1952- author.

Title: Eyewitness to crucifixion : the Romans, the cross, and the sacrifice of Jesus / Stephen M. Miller.

Description: Grand Rapids, MI : Our Daily Bread Publishers, 2020. | Includes bibliographical references and index. | Summary: "Best-selling journalist Stephen M. Miller shines a fascinating spotlight on eyewitness testimonies of Roman crucifixion. Paraphrased into casual English and accompanied by artistic interpretations, these quotations provide the historical context that surrounds the cross—an ancient Roman method of execution and the centerpiece of Christian faith"— Provided by publisher.

Identifiers: LCCN 2019045230 | ISBN 9781640700017 (paperback)

Subjects: LCSH: Crucifixion—Rome--History. | Jesus Christ—Crucifixion. | Christianity.

Classification: LCC HV8569 .M55 2020 | DDC 232.96/3—dc23

LC record available at https://lccn.loc.gov/2019045230

Printed in the United States of America

20 21 22 23 24 25 26 27 / 8 7 6 5 4 3 2 1

I was there when it happened. I have written it down. I wanted a record of our martyred Savior's power, the power of Jesus Christ. That's because it was His power on display when these martyrs died. . . . Some were crucified in the normal way— the method used for crucifying criminals. But others were crucified in a way that's viciously cruel. They were nailed to the cross upside down and then kept alive until they starved to death.

Eusebius, *Church History*

———

Would anyone willingly choose to be fastened to that cursed tree, especially after the beating that left him deathly weak, deformed, swelling with vicious welts on shoulders and chest, and struggling to draw every last, agonizing breath? Anyone facing such a death would plead to die rather than mount the cross.

Seneca, *Moral Letters*

CONTENTS

PART 2: WHAT ROMANS SAID ABOUT JESUS'S CRUCIFIXION

PART 3: WHAT THE BIBLE SAYS ABOUT JESUS'S CRUCIFIXION

IN THE DAYS OF CRUCIFIXION

Note: Some dates are approximate.

44 BC
Julius Caesar
assassinated

700s BC
Homer in *Iliad*,
Odyssey uses
Greek word
stauros for "pole"
(Bible uses it
for "cross")

519 BC
Persian King
Darius I crucifies
3,000 political
enemies

76 BC
Cicero sues
governor
who crucified
Roman citizen

700 BC   100 BC   ◄ BC │ AD

88 BC
Jewish King
Alexander
Jannaeus
crucifies 800
Pharisees

27 BC
Democratic
Roman Republic
ends; dicta-
torial Roman
Empire starts

73 BC
Romans crucify 6,000
of Spartacus's army

701 BC
Assyrians impale
Judeans after
Siege of Lachish

AD 30–33
Jesus crucified

AD 60–100
Gospel writers
use Greek
word *stauros*
for what Bibles
translate as
"cross"

AD 66
Jews start
war of inde-
pendence,
Nero report-
edly blames
Christians for
Rome fire

AD 70
Romans crush
Jewish revolt,
destroy Jerusalem,
crucify hundreds

AD 30

70

AD 46
Paul starts his
first mission trip

AD 64
Romans reportedly
crucify Peter,
behead Paul

AD 65
Nero orders
Seneca to
kill himself

AD 68
Nero kills
himself

AD 90
Roman historian
Josephus reports
crucifixion of Jesus

AD 303
Diocletian targets
Christians in The
Great Persecution
(303–311)

AD 337
Constantine
bans
crucifixion

AD 80

300

AD 110
Roman historian
Tacitus reports
on Christians and
founder Christus

AD 79
Mt. Vesuvius
destroys Pompeii

AD 313
Emperor Constantine
legalizes Christianity

PREFACE

You can thank YouTube
for this book

YouTube raised this book from the dead.

I thought I had a great idea for a book: what Romans said about crucifixions they saw.

Nobody wanted it.

My agent pitched it to a carefully selected list of editors. But the polite rejection notes said the topic sounded boring, cerebral, and best suited for professors and preachers. One editor suggested the topic might work for one of his series, written for scholars by scholars.

That eliminated me as either writer or reader.

I'm not a prof, preacher, or scholar of any sort. I'm just a former newspaper reporter who went to seminary so I could learn to write about the Bible. I'm a layman, like most folks. So I know boring when I see it.

This stuff isn't boring.

I had read what Romans wrote about crucifixions they saw. I found the ancient descriptions engaging. Jaw-dropping at times. Really. My jaw dropped. I caught myself picking it up.

I had figured if I wrote the book in easy-reading, fast-paced magazine style, paraphrasing the ancient quotes into casual English, it could interest almost anyone who wanted to know how Jesus died—and about what kind of death hounded the disciples and all the other Christians off and on for three hundred years.

After that first pitch failed to find a home for the book, we shelved it.

I figured it was dead, especially since my agent didn't seem all that eager about it in the first place.

WHEN NO ONE WANTS YOUR STUFF, THERE'S YOUTUBE

I had ten thousand words that interested no one but me—a 37-page book proposal with sample chapters that represented several weeks of my life, my research, and my writing.

I had dug up some wrenching quotes two thousand years old. They came from people who weren't in the Bible, yet they substantiated the Bible and added insight into the torture Jesus suffered.

The quotes are so old they're brand new to almost everyone, even many scholars. These eyewitness accounts are raw, vivid, and sober. I couldn't just sit on that.

So I spent several more weeks writing a video script, gathering free images, and buying the rights to other images, along with rights to some music.

I didn't think of it as an investment. I wasn't plotting to resurrect a dead book. I was simply doing what I've felt compelled to do throughout my career as an easy-reading Bible reference writer: find something worth the telling, then try to tell it well.

I called my homemade YouTube video, "What Romans Said about Crucifixion."

After a few months, the video caught a wave. It went viral. Over a million views.

I still have no idea why. I'm a rookie at video production, and this video is a one-man show, and it shows.

When I saw the number of views take a giant leap, I took the book idea back to my agent and asked if he thought it was worth a second effort.

He agreed to pitch it again. We showcased the number of YouTube video views along with the viewer engagement: more than 5,000 comments at the time.

In one of those comments, someone said something like this (though more crudely): "I can't believe an idiot like this gets a million views!"

To which I replied, "A million and one."

Here's to YouTube, with a grateful Like.

ROMAN WORDS IN CASUAL ENGLISH

The ancient quotes you read here aren't going to show up anywhere else.

I've tried to paraphrase the archaic words into easy-reading English.

I confess that I don't read Latin or Greek—at least not without the word-for-word help I get from geeky Bible reference resources such as interlinears, which I use a lot. But I do read academese. I pronounce that "ACK uh duh MEES." It's a word I use kindly to describe the writing style of many, perhaps most—if not all—scholars. I may have just exaggerated. But not by much.

Scholars, generally, are the folks who have translated the ancient Roman quotes into English. Plenty of those translations were done a century ago, or longer. They're often hard to understand, and not at all the way most folks talk today.

Some are as hard to figure out as Shakespeare.

Forsooth. Cometh on. Wouldst I forswear to thee? Nay. Mine own w'rd is mine own bond. Trusteth me as thee wouldst trusteth thy own fair loveth.

Scholars are goldmines of wonderful insight. But, unlike journalists, they often write only for each other. A journalist will pick a short, commonly used word. A scholar digs for a longer and more precise word, one that conveys a subtle message that fellow scholars will pick up on, even if no one else does. A journalist leads with the most intriguing fact, to hook the reader's attention. A scholar buries the best material deep inside an article or a book. They want to explain the entire process that led to the big idea before they unveil the big idea.

I'm a newspaper journalist who converted to Christian writing by following up my news journalism degree with a seminary degree. Since then, I've spent most of my nearly half-century career translating Bible scholars into easy-reading English. This book is a stretch because I'm translating Bible scholars along with history scholars. (My apologies to all of them for presuming to do so.)

I've done the best I can to express the ancient ideas in today's casual English. But I've also given you the references you need to look up the scholarly, more literal translations of the ancient Greek and Latin quotes. Many of those resources are freely available online, and not too difficult to locate; for example, when you see "*History of Alexander the Great*, 7.5.40–41" that refers to book 7, chapter 5, sections 40–41.

WHAT THEY SAID ABOUT CRUCIFIXION

206 BC
"I'll be buried on the cross. That's where they buried everyone in my family. My father. My grandfather. . . . It's the family tomb." Plautus, *The Braggart Soldier*, a play

45 BC
"Oh please, save your [crucifixion threats] for those purple-robed members of your royal court. It makes no difference to Theodorus whether he rots on the ground or in the air." Cicero, *Tusculan Disputations*

20 BC
"If the slave says, 'I haven't killed anyone,' then I'd say, 'Good. We don't have to hang you on a cross and feed you to those scavenger crows.'" Horace, *Epistles*

AD 64
"Officials arrested everyone who admitted to being a Christian. . . . [Some] were nailed to crosses or burned alive as human torches to light the nighttime entertainment." Tacitus, *Annals*

◄ BC | AD ►

80 BC
"The very word *cross* should be forbidden in the presence of a Roman citizen. Romans shouldn't have to think of a cross, see a cross, or hear the miserable word." Cicero, *For Rabirius on Charge of Treason*

70 BC
"Publius Gavius, whom you crucified, was a Roman citizen. . . . And you, Verres, admit it. You actually confirm that he screamed he was a Roman citizen. But it didn't make any difference to you, did it?" Cicero, *Against Verres*

AD 40–45
"I see right in front of me different kinds of crosses. . . . Some hang their victims upside down. Some impale them. . . . Others stretch out their arms onto forked poles." Seneca, *Dialogues*, To Marcia on Consolation

AD 65

"Would anyone willingly choose to be fastened to that cursed tree, especially after the beating that left him deathly weak, deformed, swelling with vicious welts on shoulders and chest, and struggling to draw every last, agonizing breath?" Seneca, *Moral Letters*

AD 90s

"About this time a wise man called Jesus appeared. . . . Pilate sentenced him to death by crucifixion." Josephus, *Antiquities of the Jews*

AD 197

"When [Christians] try to explain the reason for their rituals, they end up talking about a man executed for crimes so vile that he was hung on a wooden cross." Marcus Minucius Felix, *Octavius*

AD 200

"She set out all the usual fixings of witchcraft. . . . There were human body parts as well . . . and flesh still stuck to the nails from a cross." Apuleius, *Metamorphoses*

AD 70

"Every day Roman soldiers caught 500 Jews or more. . . . Soldiers, driven by their hatred of the Jews, nailed them to crosses. . . . [They nailed the Jews] in many different positions to entertain themselves." Josephus, *War of the Jews*

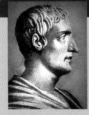

AD 110

"Christians . . . got their name from Christus. . . . One of our governors, procurator Pontius Pilate, sentenced him to death." Tacitus, *Annals*

AD 313

"They were nailed to the cross upside down and then kept alive until they starved to death." Eusebius, *Church History*

SICILY'S LAMENT. Icarus lies fallen, a bronze statue in Sicily. Inspiration for the art came from the story of a man who built wings from feathers and wax, and then flew too close to the sun, which melted the wax. This statue is a sampling of the style of art that Sicily's governor, Gaius Verres, confiscated from artists and temples. He did it to expand his fiscal portfolio. Lawyer Cicero busted him.

INTRODUCTION

'**ve** read just about every ancient Roman quote that scholars have found on crucifixion. Now, I'd like to make a suggestion.

If you want to know what some Romans thought about this form of execution, and you want to know *right now*, read the court case of Rome vs. Gaius Verres. Verres was a tumor of a governor who pillaged the wealth of Sicily (see pages 45–52).

A young and ambitious prosecutor named Cicero—The Cicero— masterfully and lyrically disassembled Governor Verres for crucifying a Roman citizen and for committing crimes of corruption. This case went to trial about seventy years before Jesus was born.

CICERO (106–43 BC)

During the trial, Cicero said cru- cifixion was a death too grisly and torturous for anyone honorable enough to be called a "Roman citizen." As he put it, crucifixion kills people "in a manner so miserable and excruci- ating that it's fit for no one but slaves."

"The very word *cross*," Cicero later wrote, "should be forbidden in the presence of a Roman citizen. Romans shouldn't have to think of a cross, see a cross, or hear the miserable word. It's unbecoming and far below a free citizen."

The defendant, Governor Verres, apparently had something against a Roman citizen and businessman named Publius Gavius. But Cicero argued there wasn't a shred of evidence that Gavius had committed any crime.

Cicero described how Verres tortured and crucified Gavius:

> He orders the man held in place, stripped, and tied up. Right there in the middle of the forum. Then he ordered someone to get the rods, in preparation to beat him. . . . He orders the man violently beaten all over his body. Again, your honors, this is in the middle of the forum of Messana that a Roman citizen was beaten with rods. . . .
>
> What about the fire, the red-hot burning plates, and all the other tools of torture? Why did you do this? If the man's begging and pitiful wailing couldn't stop you, weren't you moved even in the slightest by the groaning and crying of the Roman citizens who were watching this? How dare you drag a Roman citizen to the cross?. . . .
>
> It wasn't just Gavius who was tortured and nailed to that cross. It wasn't just one Roman citizen. Nailed to that cross was the very idea of what it means to be a free Roman citizen.

HOW TO CRUCIFY. Roman writers reporting crucifixions didn't usually describe the process in enough detail for anyone today to draw a picture of it. Surprisingly, Bible writers didn't either. The generic words they used to describe the crucifixion device could mean a T-shaped cross, a pole, or even a tree.

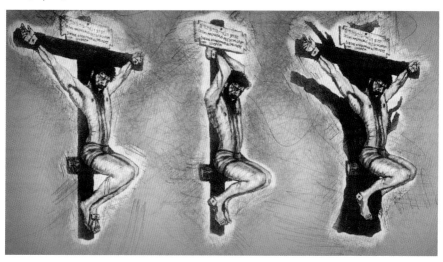

HOW ABOUT "SUSPENSION" INSTEAD OF "CRUCIFIXION"?

If we saw someone tied to a tree trunk and left to die with their feet dangling above the ground, we'd call that a crime. But we probably wouldn't call it a crucifixion.

Yet it could have been, some Christian scholars would argue.

Crucifixion methods were that diverse, they say. And for that reason, some scholars suggest we stop using "crucifixion" to describe what happened to Jesus and to others in Roman times. The word *crucifixion* instantly paints a picture in our head. We see someone nailed—hands and feet—to a T-shaped cross.

Yet when Romans wrote about what we call crucifixion, their descriptions were often so nondescript that all we know for sure is that the person was somehow hung above the ground and left to die. Nailed to a pole. Tied to a tree. Impaled on a stake.

That's why some suggest a broader and more generic word for this method of execution: suspension.

Granted, that's a word without a picture. We can't see it in our mind's eye.

But those scholars argue that in the execution of Jesus and of others hung above the ground, what we've got is a hanging without a detailed description. So why not use a generic word that reflects what little we know?

While that's the argument, it's not the prevailing view.

CRUCIFIXION CHECKLIST

There are four gotta-have-it marks of a crucifixion. Many Christian scholars seem to agree on that much. If an execution doesn't hit all four, it's not a crucifixion, strictly defined.

- ✓ **Suspension**—The victim is hanging above the ground.
- ✓ **Execution**—That's the goal, whether the victim dies or not.
- ✓ **Wood**—It might be a board or pole, with or without a crossbeam; and the victim is attached to it, whether tied or nailed.
- ✓ **Slow death**—The plan is to prolong suffering.

SUSPENDED. Romans crucified people in different ways, not necessarily with nails or a T-shaped cross. Some scholars suggest we stop using the word *crucifixion* to describe these executions. Instead, they suggest calling them *suspensions*, since the one fact that's consistent is that the victims were suspended above the ground.

Some scholars who pitch this definition say there are hardly any executions in ancient literature that even qualify as crucifixion. The ancients simply didn't give us enough details about the method of execution.

Even the Bible comes up short on the description, they'd say.

Some scholars, most notably Swedish pastor and University of Gothenburg lecturer Gunnar Samuelsson, point out that what the Gospels (the Bible books of Matthew, Mark, Luke, and John) tell us about the suspension of Jesus is limited:

1. Jesus carried to his execution site something that can be translated as either a pole, a stake, or maybe even a crossbeam, but not a T-shaped cross. The translation of the Greek word for what he carried, *stauros* (Luke 23:26), is debated.

2. After his resurrection he had wounds on his hands.

Implications in John 20:25–27 and Colossians 2:14 are that nails caused the wounds; but none of the four gospel writers mentioned nails when they described the crucifixion. (This can be confusing, because when we read some Bible translations of the crucifixion, the word "nailed" is used—in Matthew 27:35, for example. Bible translators sometimes presume the nails, but all that shows up in the original Greek language is *stauros*, which is why other Bible translations say "crucified him.")

Just about everything else that Christians think the Bible says about the crucifixion or suspension of Jesus is based on presumption, church tradition, or Old Testament prophecies written as poetry, these scholars explain. (See part 3, page 155, What the Bible Says about Jesus's Crucifixion.)

The crucifixion debate spins around a few 2,000-year-old words and how to interpret them. Here's the problem with that discussion. Words aren't solid. They're liquid. Shapeshifters. They mean one thing to one generation and another thing to the next. "Awful" originally meant "full of awe" or "awe-inspiring." Today it describes the price of printer ink. "Wasted" used to mean "worn out." But I stopped using it that way after my son and son-in-law laughed at me and said it means "drunk." Holy moly, I've never been drunk.

Clearly, we need to define a few terms so we can at least agree on what we're talking about. Even if we don't come to the same conclusions about what it all means.

CLASSIC CRUCIFIXION. When someone says "crucifixion," a picture like this is what comes to mind for many folks. But this isn't how the gospel writers described Jesus's crucifixion. They didn't provide many details. They didn't say Romans used nails to attach Jesus to the cross. The disciple Thomas presumed it when he said he wouldn't believe the Resurrection "unless I see the nail wounds in his hands" (John 20:25). Paul implied the nailing when he said that Jesus canceled our sin debt "by nailing it to the cross" (Colossians 2:14).

CRUCIFIXION DICTIONARY

CROSS (*stauros*, Greek; *crux*, Latin; *stipes*, Latin for vertical wooden pole or beam). A wooden object to which an executioner attached people, often by ropes or nails, and left them suspended above the ground to die. The single-pole *stipes* could be sharpened and used to impale someone. Or it could become the vertical part of a T-shaped cross.

Gospel writers describe the cross of Jesus as a *stauros*. This word, many scholars agree, could describe just about any wooden object to which a person could be attached: a pole, board, tree, or the T-shaped cross that early church writers linked to the execution of Jesus about a hundred years after the fact.

In Greek mythology, written several hundred years before Jesus, *stauros* was just your average pole. Homer used that word in stories such as the *Iliad* and *Odyssey* to talk about a pole or a fencepost or a piece of wood that looked like a board for a picket fence.

That's why some students of history argue that Romans crucified Jesus on a single stake, not on a cross.

But by Roman times, the word had apparently already started to

THE CROSS IN A PIGPEN. The word Bible writers used to describe the cross of Jesus, *stauros*, is the same Greek word Homer (left) used to describe the stakes a pig herder used to build a pigpen in the *Odyssey*, the epic story of Odysseus traveling home after the Trojan War and the fall of Troy (14.1). Scholars suppose that by Roman times the word had grown to mean more.

morph. *Stauros* meant "pole," sure enough. But scholars say that Roman writers also used the word to mean the upright stake in a T-shaped cross used to crucify people. And some Romans even seemed to use the word to refer to various parts of the entire instrument of execution, whether it was just an upright stake or a T-shaped cross or just the crossbar that executioners would add to a stake already planted in the ground.

It seems Romans used the word that broadly.

We do the same kind of thing.

"I'm going to nail you." That can have various meanings:

> "I'm going to catch you in the act."
> "I'm going to kill you."
> "I'm going to have my way with you."
> "I'm going to take a nail gun to your person."

Three of those are felonies.

Some scholars argue that since the Bible writers say Romans hung Jesus on a *stauros*, he likely died on a pole, not on a cross. They insist the word hadn't yet morphed from "pole" to a T-shaped "cross."

Other scholars say there's plenty of evidence that the word had changed because some Roman writers used the word that way.

It's a fairly new debate, but ongoing.

Exhibit A. There's 2,000-year-old picture evidence of crucifixion on a T-shaped cross, thanks to some folks who defaced property with graffiti (see "The cross in 2,000-year-old visual art," pages 179–183). The Roman pictures are known by where they were found in Italy: Puteoli, a city on the outskirts of Naples; and Palatine, a hill in Rome.

Exhibit B. There's also a gemstone engraved with a crucified person that many scholars identify as the first known picture of the crucified Jesus (see page 182).

Exhibit C. Surprisingly, another piece of evidence comes from a book dedicated to a Roman governor who met the apostle Paul.

The writer was Seneca, an advisor to Emperor Nero. Seneca dedicated the book, *On Anger*, to his little brother Gallio in about AD 45. That was around six years before Gallio tossed out a court case that some Jews brought against Paul. Gallio was governor of the Roman province of Achaia in what is now the southern half of Greece.

Jews accused Paul of teaching people to break the Jewish laws. Gallio threw the case out, saying, "'Listen, you Jews, if this were a case involving some wrongdoing or a serious crime, I would have a reason to accept your case. But since it is merely a question of words and names and your Jewish law, take care of it yourselves. I refuse to judge such matters.' And he threw them out of the courtroom" (Acts 18:14–16).

Seneca, writing in Rome's native language of Latin, briefly mentioned a man getting crucified with arms outstretched. The phrase in Latin reads *cruce membra distendere*, literally translated "cross limbs stretched out." It essentially means crucified with arms outstretched.

> If you decide to take a good look at what comes of anger and the trouble it causes, you'll discover this. Anger has decimated the human race more than any plague. . . . You'll see leaders show up in our history who suffered a terrible fate because of it.
>
> Anger stabbed one man in his bed.
>
> It beat another to death—while the sacred rights of hospitality should have protected him.
>
> It tore another to pieces right in front of the laws that should have protected him, within sight of the crowded forum.
>
> It forced another to die at the hands of his own son—a son murdering his dad.
>
> It killed a member of the royal court by having a slave cut his throat.
>
> It led another to a cross, where he stretched out his arms.
>
> *On Anger*, 1.2

Exhibit D. Another piece of evidence comes from a satire by Lucian. An author in the AD 100s, he used the Greek word *stauros* to describe a cross designed in the shape of the Greek letter T, called *Tau* (pronounced a bit like *towel*, but skip the "l").

> People royally cuss King Cadmus [a character in Greek mythology who is credited with introducing the Greek alphabet]. They com-

plain and wail because he added *Tau* to the alphabet. They say they're upset because tyrants used the shape of a *Tau* as a design for connecting beams of timber. Then they took what they built in the shape of that *Tau* and crucified people on it.

It's Cadmus's fault. He's the one who gave this sorry instrument of torture its sorry name [*stauros = cross*].

Given what I've just said, don't you think the *Tau* deserves to die a thousand deaths?

Consonants at Law, Sigman vs. Tau

CROSSBAR (*patibulum*, Latin; *gibbet*, Old English). Wooden beam that forms the top of a T-shaped cross used to crucify people. A Roman linguist named Nonius Marcellus (AD 300s) described it as the long, thick board that people used in ancient times to "bar the door shut." Executioners sometimes forced the condemned folks to carry it to the execution site. Ancient pictures and written descriptions suggest that during crucifixion, some executioners nailed or tied the arms of the victim to this beam and set the beam on top of a vertical stake.

When Bible writers had to describe what most Bible experts seem to think was the crossbar that Jesus carried to his execution, they had to translate into Greek the word Romans used to describe the beam. The Roman word, written in their language of Latin, is *patibulum*. But for Greek, the international

BAR THE DOOR. One Roman writer described the crossbar at the top of crucifixion crosses as boards like those used to bar the door shut from inside a house or a courtyard.

language of the day, Bible writers chose *stauros*, which people often used to describe a vertical pole or sometimes the entire cross.

Bible writers wouldn't have been the only ones who used the word to describe the crossbeam. So did Roman writers such as Macrobius (AD 370–430). He said the *patibulum*, or crossbar, was Latin for the Greek word *stauros* (*Macrobius* 1.10, AD 395).

In time, both words came to mean the entire cross.

When Matthew reports that the Romans drafted Simon from Cyrene to haul a piece of execution timber for Jesus, Matthew called it a *stauros*, presumably referring to at least part of a cross. It's not clear, in Matthew's description, if that was an entire T-shaped cross, just the vertical post, or a crossbar.

CRUCIFIXION (*stauroo, systauroo, anaskolopizo*, Greek). Nailing, tying, impaling, or in some other way attaching a person to an object such as a cross, pole, or tree—and then leaving them there, suspended, to die.

Writers seldom described the execution in enough detail to let readers today know which scenario they had in mind. So, scholars look for context clues. One clue that it's not impaling: the crucified person lives long enough to carry on a conversation. A person impaled in the torso or up the posterior and through the throat probably died quickly.

LOTS OF CRUCIFIXIONS, FEW NAMES OF VICTIMS

Scholars have tallied at least 30,000 individuals crucified by the Romans, based on surviving reports. But there are only 20 names of crucified individuals that have survived in existing sources.

SUSPENSION (see Greek words for "crucifixion"). Method of slow execution that involves dangling a victim above the ground.

What a surprise. We thought we knew what crucifixion was. We had the picture in our head. Yet when we read what Romans themselves said about crucifixions they saw with their own eyes, we discover than one picture isn't nearly enough.

WHAT'S THE POINT OF THIS BOOK?

That's a question the editor asked me to answer for you, as though I could.

You're going to have to pick your own point.

I can tell you why I decided to spend the better part of a year of my life working fulltime on this book:

- This stuff was new to me. I've worked four decades writing Bible study books, and I had overlooked this.

- Crucifixion scenes the Romans described are so engaging and graphic that I found myself caught up in the history of it all, much like when I read eyewitness accounts of a war or a battle.

ROMAN DESCRIPTIONS OF A CROSS

A beam of wood planted straight up from the ground is just part of a cross, though the largest part. But the cross that people associate with we Christians is a complete cross. It comes with a crossbeam and plank as a seat [to prolong the torture].

Tertullian, *To the Nations* (*Ad Nationes*), 1.12

I see right in front of me different kinds of crosses made by different people. Some hang their victims upside down. Some impale them through the private parts. Others stretch out their arms onto forked poles.

Seneca, *Dialogues*, To Marcia on Consolation, 6.20

[Roman Emperor] Augustus sent for Eros and asked him if it was true. Did he eat the champion quail?

Eros admitted it.

Augustus crucified him—nailed him to a ship's mast.

Plutarch, *Sayings of Romans*

They were nailed to the cross upside down and then kept alive until they starved to death.

Eusebius, *Church History* 6.2–4; 7.2; 8.1–2

PETER'S CRUCIFIXION. "Peter was crucified at Rome with his head down, which is the way he wanted to suffer." A church leader named Origin wrote that in the AD 200s. An earlier leader, Clement, wrote in a letter sometime between AD 80 and AD 98 that Peter died a martyr.

- Among the thousands the Romans crucified, there was one in particular. Jesus.

History is enough of a point for some readers, myself included. I love reading history, especially history from Bible times.

But it's the death of Jesus that gives life to this book.

That might seem odd to non-Christian readers because pitifully few Romans even mentioned him. Yet we Christians read Jesus into every graphic description of a crucified soul. We can't help it. It's a bit like reading about someone dying of the same cancer that killed our wife or husband or child. We read of the other soul's suffering and we remember what our loved one suffered.

The death of Jesus, oddly, became the beating heart of every Christian. It's the only thing Paul said was worth bragging about: "I will never brag about anything except the cross of our Lord Jesus Christ" (Galatians 6:14 CEV).

We brag about heroes who died to save others. We count Jesus among those heroes.

Yet in his death, there's more. He's alive. Even one of the first-century Roman writers, Josephus, said the disciples of Jesus were convinced of this.

Within two months of the Crucifixion, one of his disciples, Peter, preached a sermon about the resurrected Jesus. And he did it right in front of the Jewish leaders who had orchestrated the death of Jesus.

If there's such a thing as a birthday of the Christian church, that day has to be a contender.

The history of Roman crucifixion is a fine reason, I hope, for me to write this book and for others to read it. But the crucifixion of Jesus is the only reason this book made it to publication.

His death lit the fire.

We don't know exactly what Jesus suffered from start to finish. So, when we read what someone else suffered, we wonder if Jesus suffered it, too.

PART 1

WHAT ROMANS SAID ABOUT CRUCIFIXION

SENECA SCULPTURE, early AD 200s

CHAPTER 1

"WORST TORTURE OF ALL"

—SENECA THE YOUNGER
(ABOUT 4 BC–AD 65)

Philosopher, playwright, and advisor to Nero,
and the Roman emperor who launched
the empire-wide persecution of Christians

Romans dreamed up gruesome ways to execute people. Seneca, in letters and essays, testified as an eyewitness who wrote about what he saw:

- Two chariots tied onto people and then driven in opposite directions to pull them apart.

- Victims taking "fire in the mouth," perhaps molten metal or flammable material touched off by a torch.

- Executioners tying people into a leather sack, typically with a snake, monkey, dog, and rooster. Quite the punitive cocktail. They tossed sack and all into the Tiber River, where everything inside drowned.

The worst torture of all, Seneca wrote, was crucifixion.

Seneca spent more than a dozen years advising Nero—the nasty Roman emperor who jumpstarted the persecution of Christians by condemning them to die as entertainment in Rome's arena. He killed

NERO TO SENECA: "DIE"

Lucius Annaeus Seneca served as young Nero's tutor and later as Emperor Nero's speechwriter and chief advisor—until Nero ordered him to commit suicide.

That wasn't the first time a boss told Seneca to kill himself. It was the third. And last. Emperor Caligula was first. The Roman Senate sentenced him to death, too.

BORN RICH

Seneca the Younger got his nickname from his dad, Seneca the Elder, an exceptional teacher of public speaking. He lived in Rome.

Not surprisingly, Seneca studied public speaking. Philosophy, too.

Respiratory problems sailed him south to the dry weather of Egypt. There, he gradually recovered while staying with his aunt, who was married to a governor.

Seneca came back to Rome at about the age of thirty-five, launching a career in politics and law. It didn't take long for him to somehow offend Emperor Caligula, who ordered him to commit suicide. Advisors talked Caligula out of that, with assurances that Seneca was unhealthy and would soon die. Didn't happen.

About ten years into Seneca's career, at roughly the age of forty-five, the Senate sentenced him to death. Senators did it because Emperor Claudius's wife—the reliably unreliable Messalina—accused him of adultery with a woman Messalina had political reasons to mess with. Claudius reduced the sentence, merely banishing Seneca to the island of Corsica. That's where he started writing.

ADVISOR TO THE EMPEROR

Messalina managed to get herself executed for plotting a coup against her husband.

Emperor Claudius's new wife convinced her husband to recall Seneca to Rome in AD 49. The next year, Seneca got the job of praetor, a judicial official with a seat on the Senate. He also won the honor of tutoring the emperor's adopted son, the future Emperor Nero.

Seneca wrote a wonderful eulogy for Nero to deliver at the funeral of Claudius, who was murdered in AD 54. Seneca also wrote Nero's first public speech, promising freedom and justice for all people, not just for the rich and influential.

Wishful thinking. But for several years, Seneca was able to help suppress Nero's dark side.

When Nero murdered his mother, the woman who had lobbied for Seneca's return to Rome, Seneca found himself in the awk-

ward position of having to justify it as an execution. He tried to retire, but Nero wouldn't let him. So Seneca pulled back from public life as much as possible, and during that time he wrote some of his most famous works, including *Moral Letters to Lucilius*.

In AD 65, at about age 70, he was accused—many historians say falsely—of taking part in a plot against Nero. By this time, the emperor had gone so far to the dark side that he would have needed the Star of Bethlehem to find his way out. Nero was deeply depressed and angry. A year earlier, much of Rome had burned to the ground in a mysterious fire that many blamed on him.

Nero ordered Seneca to kill himself. It was an order Nero gave to many top officials. Seneca, true to his matter-of-fact Stoic philosophy and to his depraved emperor, cut his wrists and bled out. Some reports say he bled too slowly, and an attending soldier finished him off.

SURPRISING FACTS

Seneca's older brother, Gallio, governor of the province of Achaia in southern Greece, met the apostle Paul. Gallio heard Jews make charges against the traveling preacher in about AD 52. Gallio threw the case out, saying the dispute was over religious rules: "I refuse to judge such matters" (Acts 18:15).

Seneca's younger brother became the father of Lucan, famed poet.

This was a high-profile family. Until Nero. All three brothers were ordered to commit suicide. They all opened their arteries and bled to death.

them in various ways, including crucifixion. What Seneca saw during those years gave him something to write about during his retirement. He wrote essays, letters, and even stage plays.

Seneca, in a letter, wrote one of the most graphic and wrenching descriptions of Roman crucifixion that has survived.

The letter is one of 124 in a collection called *Moral Letters to Lucilius*, whom Seneca describes as governor of Sicily, an island off the southern coast of Italy. No one today seems to know if Lucilius was a real person. There's no record of anyone by that name serving as Sicily's governor at the time.

Whether Lucilius was real or fictional, the letters follow a theme familiar to Roman citizens—how to be a good Stoic. Stoics said everything that happens to us is determined by the Force that controls creation. They argue that our best response is to control our harmful emotions. Cue First Officer Spock, of the Starship Enterprise.

Packaging this theme as a collection of letters to Lucilius, some say, may have been Seneca's technique for personalizing his message. This made it easier for readers to follow along in what sounds like a correspondence course in philosophy.

Regardless of his intent with *Moral Letters*, Seneca left us a stark commentary on crucifixion. The casual way in which he weaves crucifixion into a conversation about something else entirely hints at how common it was.

Seneca seems to have nothing but disgust for crucifixion.

This is Seneca, paraphrased into casual English:

> Dear Lucilius.
>
> Here's what I suggest. Live each day like it's the only day you'll ever get—one entire lifetime in 24 hours. Folks who carefully plan a well-rounded day can relax and enjoy the day. But some people plan nothing. They simply hope the day turns out okay. It doesn't. It slips away—lost to greed and to the fear of death.
>
> Remember that worthless prayer of Maecenas? He was so afraid of dying that he said he'd rather suffer anything else: energy-sapping disease, deformity, even crucifixion—the worst pain of all. His prayer went like this:

Create me a hand that shakes with palsy.
Set me on feet too weak to carry me, then call me a cripple.
Build a crooked hump and slap it on my back.
Shake my teeth so loose that they rattle inside my head.
It's okay as long as I'm alive.
Save me, save me, I'm begging you.
Even if it's to sit nailed on a cross.

There he is, praying for the worst torture on earth. He prays to suffer, as though that's any way to live. He would be a pitiful soul if he got what he prayed for and lived long enough to suffer crucifixion.

"No way," he says. "Sap my strength, but keep me breathing in my broken bag of bones. Cripple me if you want. Just let me live—with a body busted up and disfigured if need be. A little more time on earth is all I ask. Go ahead if you have to, set me on a cross and nail me there!"

Is life worth the pain of hanging nailed on a stake merely to postpone what will cure the pain and end the punishment? Is it really worth this price to buy the breath we will have to give away? . . .

Tell me, is Death as bad as that? He asks for the worst torture of all. . . .

BEATING JESUS. Whips tear into the back of Jesus, in a beating that gospel writers say Roman Governor Pilate ordered. Seneca, advisor to Emperor Nero, wrote that crucifixion beatings were so intense that they left the victim "deathly weak, deformed, swelling with vicious welts on shoulders and chest, and struggling to draw every last, agonizing breath."

Is there really such a thing as a person who would prefer wasting away in pain on a cross—dying limb by limb one drop of blood at a time—rather than dying quickly?

Would anyone willingly choose to be fastened to that cursed tree, especially after the beating that left him deathly weak, deformed, swelling with vicious welts on shoulders and chest, and struggling to draw every last, agonizing breath? Anyone facing such a death would plead to die rather than mount the cross.

Moral Letters, 101.10–14

MERCY WORKS BETTER THAN PUNISHMENT

Roman Emperor Nero was eighteen years old and new on the job when Seneca wrote him some wonderful essays on the merits of mercy.

Ten years later, Nero ordered Seneca to commit suicide.

The emperor accused him, wrongly many historians say, of taking part in a plot to kill him.

That's ironic, of course, not only because Nero—tutored in mercy—showed no mercy to his tutor but because Nero earned fame for not showing mercy to much of anyone.

For heaven's sake, the guy killed his own mother, Agrippina the Younger, who didn't get any older. It took him two tries. Then he killed his wife. He allegedly killed his second wife, too.

But he's perhaps best remembered for blaming Christians for the AD 64 fire that burned much of Rome. That's when he launched the first emperor-approved persecution of Christians. He burned them in the arena for entertainment. And he executed them in other ways. Early church writers say it was this wave of persecution that crucified Peter and beheaded Paul.

Still, Seneca wrote some wonderful essays on the topic. In the process, he talked about crucifixion. He compared it to another horrifying method of execution: tying people inside a leather sack with wild animals and then throwing them—sack and all—into the Tiber River.

It's conceivable that an eighteen-year-old emperor might not have read a philosopher's essays on mercy, or on anything else that didn't have something to do with stuff that interests eighteen-year-old men.

If Nero didn't read the essay, here's part of what he missed:

> When you take a close look at it, you'll discover that the more you punish crime, the more crime you'll have to punish. In five years, your father executed more parent-killers—sewing them into sacks for drowning—than were executed that way since the beginning of time.
>
> . . . Parricide [killing a parent or another close relative] was unheard of until we made a law against it. This law with its penalty is what gave people the idea to commit the crime. Love of

BAG 'EM. This wasn't, perhaps, the worst way to die. But it was at least a contender. Romans called it *poena cullei*, "penalty of the sack." Romans generally reserved it for people who killed their own father or mother. Romans stuffed the criminal into a leather sack, as the first ingredient of a critter cocktail. They added one snake, one monkey, one dog, and one rooster or chicken. They sewed the bag closed and tossed it in the Tiber River. Splash.

family soon died. From the time that law was created, more people have been sacked than have died on the cross.

Where people are rarely punished, life is more innocent and peaceful. Everyone is better off because of it. . . . A nation that executes a lot of its people is as disgraceful as a doctor who has to go to the funeral of a lot of his patients.

Rulers who aren't as strict are better obeyed than stern rulers. That's because people naturally want to live by their own rules. When they see a rule someone else tells them to obey, they tend to want to break it. They don't like getting bossed around.

They would rather follow someone than get led around by them. It's the same way with horses. Well-bred, spirited horses work best with a loose rein. Mercy points people toward innocence. Citizens catch the spirit of it and decide it's the best way to live. That's why mercy works better than strict rules and stern punishment.

Dialogues, On Clemency (Mercy), 1.23

ARMS STRETCHED OUT ON FORKED POLES

Try to imagine Leonard Nimoy's stoic character, Spock of the Starship Enterprise, writing a letter of condolence to a mother whose son has died. That's fairly close to the kind of letter that Seneca, a Stoic in his Greek philosophy, wrote to Marcia. She was a grieving mother in about AD 40. That's a few years after the crucifixion of Jesus that occurred around AD 30–33.

Marcia had grieved for her son for over three years before Seneca wrote the letter of consolation. It reads like an essay for a philosophy class.

It's not clear why Seneca felt compelled to write the letter. But scholars make note of the fact that Marcia's dad, Aulus Cremutius Cordus, was an incredibly rich and influential historian.

Whatever the reason he wrote it, he missed the opportunity to show empathy. Instead, he said a lot of the kind of things grief counselors today would tell us not to say:

We understand so little about our own suffering that we don't have the sense to praise death and to look forward to it as Nature's greatest adventure. . . . It puts an end to the exhaustion of old age. It cuts down young people, blooming and full of hope. It calls the children home before they have to struggle through the hardest stages of life.

Dialogue, To Marcia on Consolation, 6.20

Oh yeah, I feel better already.

It might make sense for Spock to say something like this, and we might accept it as his most sincere effort to console, but if anyone else would say it, we might throw a punch.

Seneca, as a Stoic, taught that since we do not control our own destiny, we should embrace it.

To which a grieving mother today might say, "Embrace this," as she tags him with a slap across the face.

In the same section of his letter, Seneca said not all crucifixions looked alike. There was no pattern everyone followed. Crucifixions were as varied as the executioners performing them.

CREATIVE HANGING. Romans didn't have just one method of crucifixion. Seneca wrote, "Some hang their victims upside down. Some impale them through the private parts. Others stretch out their arms onto forked poles."

Death frees a slave in spite of the slave master's disapproval. Death breaks the chains of a captive. Death frees the prisoner locked up by a stubborn soul. . . . I see right in front of me different kinds of crosses made by different people. Some hang their victims upside down. Some impale them through the private parts. Others stretch out their arms onto forked poles.

I see ropes, whips, and tools of torture crafted for specific limbs and joints. But I see death, too. There are bloodthirsty enemies out there along with pushy citizens who think too much of themselves and too little of others. But wherever I see them, I see death as well. . . . I owe death a huge debt of gratitude. Death is the reason life is so dear to me.

Dialogue, To Marcia on Consolation, 6.20

"THEY DROVE NAILS INTO HIS SKIN"

Seneca tackles the question of evil in the world by suggesting it's not so evil after all.

He explains his philosophy in an essay that he writes in the form of a letter known as the *Dialogue of Providence*. He addresses it to a man called Lucilius, governor of Sicily:

Lucilius, you asked me a hard question: If Providence rules the world, why do so many bad things happen to good men? . . . God doesn't pet a good man. God tests him and hardens him and molds him into the kind of man God wants him to become. . . .

Let me tell you how to disgrace a gladiator. Match him with an inferior. He knows that a win without danger is a win without glory. Fortune is just like that gladiator. She matches herself with the bravest of souls. She will skip right by those people she doesn't respect. She goes straight to the most respectable and determined people. She's going to match her strength against them.

She tested Mucius by fire, Fabricius by poverty, Rutilius by exile, Regulus by torture. . . . Look at Regulus. What harm did Fortune do to him when she made him an example of good faith and enduring strength? They drove nails into his skin. Wherever he rested his weary body, it rested on a wound. They used an instrument of torture to force his eyes to stay open. But here's a fact. The more he suffered, the more he is glorified.

Do you think he regrets paying such a high price for this high honor? I'll tell you how much he does not regret it. Heal him. Heal all of his wounds and send him back into the Senate chambers. He'll tell those senators exactly the same thing he told them before. He'll give them the very same advice that got him tortured to death.

Dialogues, To Lucius on Providence, 1.3

ANGRY ENOUGH TO CRUCIFY SOMEONE

Anger has its place, some philosophers say, because people need it from time to time.

Seneca begs to differ, and he takes on Aristotle to build his argument.

Seneca says anger keeps bad company—crucifixion:

Aristotle says we need anger, and it would be terrible if we got rid of it. He says anger is the kick in the butt that we sometimes need to do the right thing. He says if we don't have a supply of anger in the arsenal of weapons we keep inside our head, we're defenseless. . . .

Well, I for one don't believe it. We need to open our eyes and take a long hard look at what anger does to people. It turns them into ferocious monsters. When one man gets enraged at another, he can go completely insane. He can destroy himself as well as his enemy. . . .

Just in case anyone is deluded enough to think there's a useful place for anger on occasion, let me point out a few examples of what anger-gone-crazy looks like.

Anger looks like the rack [a team of horses pulling people apart]. It looks like the rope, the torture chamber, and the cross. It looks like fire surrounding burning bodies. Hooks that catch and drag the living and the dead. Tools of torture. Arms and legs ripped from bodies. Branded foreheads. Dens of man-eating wild animals.

This is how anger makes itself useful. This is the company it keeps.

Anger stands, menacing and growling, more threatening and

dangerous than all these tortures because they are just weapons in anger's arsenal.

Dialogues, On Anger, addressed to Novatus, 5.3.3

THE CROSS IN AN EVIL PARADE

Seneca describes the cross as one of many featured acts in a Parade of Evil.

He seems to be painting a mental picture of a gruesome spectacle that a crowd might see in a Roman coliseum. He doesn't sound like a fan of anything that goes on there:

> Evil marches in as a huge parade, with swords and fire and chains and a troop of wild animals disemboweling people.
>
> Picture the featured acts: prison, the cross, the hook [that drags bodies and corpses through the streets]. Then there's the stake they drive up through a person until it sticks out through the throat.
>
> Go ahead, picture arms and legs ripped off by two chariots

CHRISTIAN MARTYRS' LAST PRAYER. A gruesome spectacle that a crowd might see in a Roman coliseum.

tied onto a body and pulled in opposite directions. Let's not forget clothing smeared and soaked in flammable material.

Moral Letters, To Lucilius, 14.4–5

SLAVES CRUCIFIED FOR RAPING MASTERS

Slaves could be crucified for any reason, though Seneca said people were crazy to kill slaves for minor mistakes. He lobbied for the punishment to fit the crime. For slaves who raped and killed their masters, he didn't seem willing to argue against crucifixion:

> A vicious intruder took control of a territory. He freed the slaves and then told them to go ahead and kill their masters and rape the women. Local officials and landowners ran away. That included one man who had a son, along with a daughter left behind.
>
> All the slaves raped the women of their masters, with one exception. The slave of the man with the daughter left behind refused to let anyone violate the girl. He kept her safe.
>
> After someone killed the intruder, the officials and the landowners came back. They crucified all their slaves, with one exception. The man with the loyal slave freed him and allowed him to marry the girl.
>
> The man's son, however, has formally accused his father of going insane.

Controversiae, 7.6

NO BURIAL FOR THE CRUCIFIED

Do people who kill themselves deserve a decent burial?

That's a debate Seneca says the Romans were having. In passing, Seneca also adds a note about what happens to crucified bodies:

> Everyone gets a burial. Nature makes sure of it. A wave that washes someone overboard also lowers them and covers them. Crucified bodies attached to the cross crumble and fall into their grave. As for people burned alive, fiery punishment buries them.

Controversiae, 8.4

MARCUS TULLIS CICERO. Sculpture from first century AD with painting of the ruins of Rome's Forum in the background.

CHAPTER 2

"I AM A CITIZEN OF ROME"

—CICERO (106–43 BC)

*Roman consul (highest elected office),
lawyer, and one of the Roman Empire's
most famous public speakers*

When the people of Sicily decided to sue their ex-governor, Gaius Verres, for corruption and for plundering them of money and land and art treasures, they turned to a 33-year-old lawyer on the political rise, Cicero. Rome had appointed him as a finance investigator for the region.

Earlier, Rome had appointed Verres governor of Sicily for one year, in 73 BC, but he stayed for three. That's because Rome got distracted by top-dog power struggles and several wars, including one with escaped slaves and gladiators led by Spartacus. By the time Verres left office in 76 BC, the year Cicero landed the job as investigator, Verres had grown bold enough to crucify Roman citizens. Rome had outlawed that.

More than a decade later, Cicero wrote, "The very word *cross* should be forbidden in the presence of a Roman citizen. Romans shouldn't have to think of a cross, see a cross, or hear the miserable word. It's unbecoming and far below a free citizen" (*For Rabirius on Charge of Treason*, 16).

Though Verres had the money to hire the best lawyers, Cicero's meticulous research delivered in eloquent speeches won the case.

ROME'S GREATEST PUBLIC SPEAKER TALKS HIMSELF TO DEATH

Marcus Tillius Cicero, one of the greatest public speakers in the history of the Roman Empire, didn't know how to pick a politician. It was the death of him.

Cicero was an old-school Roman, bucking the rise of would-be dictators like Julius Caesar, Pompey, Marc Antony, and Octavian, better known as Augustus. Cicero wanted to preserve the Republic—the more democratic practice of senators representing all people.

As Roman strongmen jockeyed for control of the Empire, three teamed up to form what became known as the First Triumvirate. That's not a Republic. In this case it was the Roman Empire ruled by three men: Julius Caesar, Crassus, and Pompey.

Caesar, in 60 BC, invited Cicero to accept a role under the new regime. Cicero declined.

RISE TO POWER

Cicero's family was rich, and he got a fine education. He lived in the city of Arpino, along the coastal hills between Rome and Naples. But he didn't come from a family of social and political elites. And despite his remarkable achievements, those folks never fully embraced him.

In 89 BC, while in his 20s, Cicero served in the military under General Pompey's father, Pompeius Strabo. That could help explain why he later sided with Pompey over other leaders competing for the Empire's top job.

About ten years later, Cicero started practicing law, and folks saw how brilliant he was at public speaking and at defending his clients.

That started his rise to power in politics. First public job: quaestor, in financial administration. Then on to become praetor, a judicial officer. By 63 BC, at about age 43, the Senate voted him into the highest elected office in the Empire: consul, a head of state a bit like the leader of the senate today. But with term limits. This was a one-year job.

After Cicero rejected Caesar's invitation to join the administration of the Three-Man-Rule, Cicero started working to drive a wedge

Cosa (Orbetello)
Rome
Appia
CORSICA
Tyrrhenian S
SARDINIA
Mediterranean Sea

between Pompey and Caesar. No luck. The opposite happened. Pompey eventually pressured Cicero into backing the three rulers.

Crassus died in battle trying to expand the Roman Empire deeper into the Middle East by taking on the Parthian Empire, in what is now Iran and eastern Turkey.

Caesar had been commanding an army with a lot of success in what is now France. He broke Roman law when he brought his army back home without permission. What followed was three years of civil war that ended in 45 BC with Caesar becoming the dictator.

Cicero backed out of public life and produced an incredible library of works. He wrote poetry, speeches, letters, legal disputes, and philosophy. More than 900 of his letters survive in multivolume book series.

He returned to politics after Caesar's assassination in 44 BC, but he made two fatal mistakes in judgment.

1. He advised the Senate to declare war on Marc Antony.

2. About Caesar's adopted son, Octavian, who later became known as Caesar Augustus, he said, "The young man should be given praise, distinctions—and then be disposed of."

Cicero's mistake wasn't just ending a sentence with a preposition.

He criticized two of the men who helped make up the Second Triumvirate. The third was a politician called Marcus Aemilius Lepidus.

Soldiers hunted Cicero down and found him within a day's walk of where he grew up. They took his head and hands back to Rome and put them on display at the speaker's platform in the forum, where he had once addressed the crowds in public meetings.

That served as a dramatic closing argument against the best public speaker of the time. It was a jarring message to anyone thinking of doing what Romans once took for granted—speaking freely.

Caesar Augustus outlasted the other two men and became the emperor who ruled the Empire when Jesus was born.

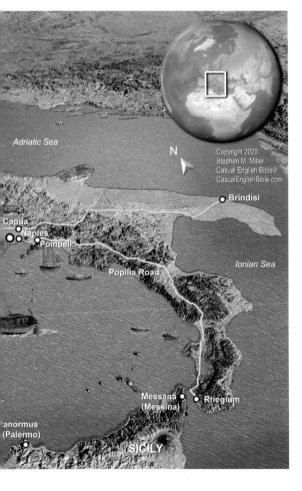

Adriatic Sea

N

Copyright 2020
Stephen M. Miller
Casual English Bible®
CasualEnglishBible.com

Brindisi

Capua
Naples
Pompeii

Popilia Road

Ionian Sea

Messana
(Messina)
Rhegium

anormus
(Palermo)

SICILY

What follows is an easy-reading paraphrase of what Cicero said about the governor who crucified a Roman citizen. Cicero's speech, wrapping up his case for the prosecution, is part of a script that fills five books now known as *Against Verres*.

I've used up almost all the words in my treasury. I've done this to show you how wicked this man is. . . . What's left for me now as I grapple with how to present a matter as important as this next one? There's just one thing left to do. I'll tell you about it, plain and simple. This matter is so important that it doesn't need an eloquent speech of introduction. Indeed, I don't have any. You're not going to need it. You're going to get upset just listening to the plain facts.

I'm talking about Publius Gavius. He was a citizen of the Roman city of Cosa [north of Rome]. He was one of a huge number of other Roman citizens Verres threw into prison. Gavius somehow escaped from the stone quarries and fled to Messana [now Messina, a coastal city in northern Sicily, four miles [6 km] from Italy, across a narrow strait of water]. He said he planned to go straight to Rome and deal with Verres there.

He didn't realize that Messana wasn't safe. Gavius was arrested and brought before the Mamertine judges. Well, it just so happened that Verres came to Messana that very day. . . .

Verres stormed into the forum, fired up with a wild temper powered by pure evil. His eyes glared. You could tell just by looking at him that something cruel was going to happen. Everyone waited to see what he would do.

Suddenly, he ordered the man held in place, stripped, and tied up. Right there in the middle of the forum. Then he ordered someone to get the rods, in preparation to beat him.

This pitiful man screamed that he was a Roman citizen—a citizen of the town of Cosa. He cried out that he had worked with Lucius Pretius, a well-known businessman and trader at the city of Panormus [modern Palermo, Italy]. He said this hoping Verres would recognize that he was telling the truth.

Instead, Verres said he had discovered that Gavius was a spy. He said leaders of runaway slaves sent him to Sicily. But there was nothing to substantiate this claim. Not a witness. Not a shred of evidence. Not the slightest suspicion in the mind of anyone but Verres.

He ordered the man violently beaten all over his body. Again, your honors, this is in the middle of the forum of Messana where a Roman citizen was beaten with rods.

The man didn't groan when they hit him. There was only one sound that came out of his mouth. Between the thunder of each blow he screamed, "I am a citizen of Rome."

He believed in the power of those words. He believed that the truth of this single statement could stop the beating and end his torture.

Well, it didn't work. Not only did it fail to stop the rods but, as he kept repeating the claim that he was a citizen, a cross—did you hear me—a cross was prepared for this pitiful man. He had no idea that someone would abuse their power by overreaching this far. It was unthinkable.

Liberty. What a sweet name it is. Roman citizenship. What an honorable privilege it is—and widely admired. . . . Have our rights as Roman citizens become so worthless that people in the

CRUCIFIED FOR TARGET PRACTICE

After Alexander the Great crushed the Persian army of Darius III (about 380–339 BC), a Persian provincial governor named Bessus launched a successful coup against Darius.

First-century Roman historian Quintus Curtius Rufus reports the story in his only surviving work, a history of Alexander.

Bessus arrested Darius and possibly helped fatally wound him with javelins. Whoever wounded him apparently left him for dead. Alexander's Greek soldiers later found Darius either dead or dying.

Alexander ordered Oxathres, brother of dead Darius, to bring Bessus to him.

Alexander had Bessus attached to a cross—after slicing off Bessus's ears and nose. Greek barbarians then used him for archery target practice.

Alexander later stationed guards by the corpse so no one would take it, not even scavenger birds.

History of Alexander the Great, 7.5.40–41

town of an allied Roman province would tie up one of our citizens in the forum and beat him with rods, at the order of a man who owes every bit of his authority to the kindness of Roman citizens?

What am I supposed to say about all of this? What about the fire, the red-hot burning plates, and all the other tools of torture? Why did you do this? If the man's begging and pitiful wailing couldn't stop you, weren't you moved even in the slightest by the groaning and crying of the Roman citizens who were watching this? How dare you drag a Roman citizen to the cross? . . .

I'm going to introduce you to citizens of Cosa and family members who will confirm for you—too late—that Publius Gavius, whom you crucified, was a Roman citizen . . . not a spy for runaway slaves. . . . My witnesses are solid. . . . I've already produced witnesses who say they saw this man dragged to the

CRUCIFIED, BUT BURIED

Buried bones of a crucified man showed up in a Jerusalem-area tomb that dates to the first century BC or AD. Archaeologist Vassilios Tzaferis excavated the tomb in 1968. One heel bone had a nail still embedded in it. There are also remnants of wood between the head of the nail and the heel bone. The wood apparently acted as a washer between the ankle and the head of the nail. This made it harder for the victim to pop through the nails and escape.

The dead man's name is apparently the one etched into the ossuary, which is a limestone box that holds the skeletal bones. Jehohanan, son of Hagakol. He's better known as "the crucified man." Both the box and the bones date to about 2,000 years ago.

Scholars debate how the executioner attached Jehohanan to the cross. One popular theory is that the executioner nailed the victim's feet through a heel and into each side of the cross, left and right.

Jehohanan's wrists and forearms weren't damaged much. Because of that, some scholars suggest the executioner tied Jehohanan's arms to a crossbeam. Other scholars point out some scratches on the arm bones, and say the executioner could have caused those by driving nails through the flesh and between the bones.

These theories are a bone of contention for at least one scholar.

"Scholars have read too much into it," says Gunnar Samuelsson, author of *Crucifixion in Antiquity*, a meticulously detailed

cross while screaming that he was a Roman citizen. And you, Verres, admit it. You actually confirm that he screamed he was a Roman citizen.

But it didn't make any difference to you, did it? There wasn't the least bit of hesitation inside that head of yours—no pause before sending this man to the cruelest and most shameful punishment of all. . . .

Your honors, I want to make sure you know that Verres erected the cross at a spot never before used for this in all of Messana's history. He picked the location because of what it allowed Gavius to see as he hung there, slowly dying in torture and agony. Gavius had a scenic view of Italy, just across the narrow strait. He could see the land of his liberty from the land that had enslaved him.

Italy, too, could watch the murder of her son, killed in a

book about crucifixion. "They have drawn too far-reaching conclusions from a heel-bone that for some reason had a large nail in it."

To which other scholars might ask, "Well, my goodness. I wonder why someone would drive a large iron nail through this man's heel? Or was this the kind of accident that sometimes happens to a drunk carpenter?"

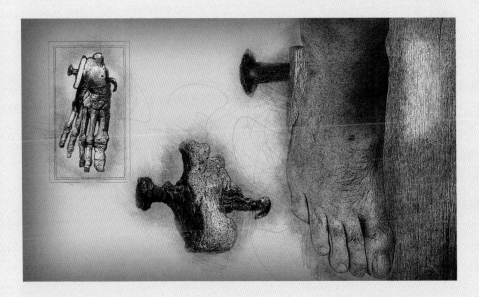

manner so miserable and excruciating that it's fit for no one but slaves.

It's a crime merely to tie up a Roman citizen. Much worse to beat him; that's evil. And to crucify him—that's almost like killing your own father or brother.

What am I supposed to say about the crucifixion of this man? I can't think of a word bad enough to describe something that's this wrong. Crucifixion wasn't punishment enough, as far as Verres was concerned. He gave the command, "Let him see his country while he dies. Let him die within eyeshot of the laws and the liberty that would have protected him."

It wasn't just Gavius who was tortured and nailed to that cross. It wasn't just one Roman citizen. Nailed to that cross was the very idea of what it means to be a free Roman citizen. . . .

The monument Verres chose to represent his audacity and pure evil was a cross he raised at the entrance into Sicily, still within sight of Italy and of all travelers sailing through the narrow strait between.

Against Verres, 5.61–66

VIEW TO DIE FOR. Cicero charged the former governor of Sicily with illegally crucifying a Roman citizen here at Messina. The governor, apparently out of spite and in a show of power, crucified the man here so that, as he hung dying, he could look across the strait and see his homeland of Italy, where he could have found protection and justice.

SNARKY REPLY TO THREAT OF CRUCIFIXION

Roman writers loved telling a Greek story about one of Alexander the Great's successors who threatened to crucify an atheist. Several writers picked up the story, apparently because they appreciated the humor, insight, and chutzpah in the atheist's response to a bullying general who had become a king.

This bully was a man named Lysimachus (360–281 BC). He ruled what are now parts of Greece and western Turkey.

The atheist was an African philosopher from what is now Libya: Theodorus (about 340–250 BC).

Theodorus's king, Ptolomy, who ruled out of Egypt, sent him on a diplomatic mission to meet with King Lysimachus.

Theodorus apparently wasn't all that diplomatic.

While on that mission, he managed to offend King Lysimachus so much that the king threatened to crucify him.

SKY BURIAL. Tibetan monks serve a corpse to birds in what is called a sky burial. When a king in Greece threatened an ambassador from Egypt with crucifixion, the ambassador wrote that he didn't care if he rotted in the air or on the ground. He also pointed out that some people actually honor their dead by serving the corpse to the birds.

Here's a paraphrase of the story, drawing from several writers:

When Lysimachus overheard Theodorus talking way too freely about atheism, Lysimachus said, "Aren't you the Theodorus who managed to get himself banished from Athens?"

"Yes, that's me," Theodorus said. "Athens couldn't handle me any more than the human woman Semele could handle giving birth to the god Bacchus."

"Don't ever come back here," Lysimachus said.

"I won't," Theodorus said. "Not unless Ptolemy sends me."

[When Lysimachus later threatened to crucify Theodorus, the philosopher reportedly wrote a terse reply.]

"Oh please, save your abominable taunts for those purple-robed members of your royal court. It makes no difference to Theodorus whether he rots on the ground or in the air. . . . In fact, the people of Bacteria [now east Afghanistan] consider it a happy ending when they bury a loved one by serving the corpse to the birds." [Called "sky burial" today, it's still practiced in Tibet.]

Tusculan Disputations by Cicero as well as writings
by Seneca, Plutarch, and Valerius Maximus

CHAPTER 3

"GOOD. WE DON'T HAVE TO HANG YOU ON A CROSS"

—HORACE (65–8 BC)

Roman poet and satirist

Horace, one of the Roman Empire's most famous poets, lived and wrote when Mary the mother of Jesus was growing up. He wasn't just a poet though. He wrote poems, satires, essays, and letters that publishers collected into books and scholars still study today.

He mentioned crucifixion in at least one letter and in a satirical poem.

In the letter, he said a slave who hadn't killed anyone didn't need to worry about getting crucified and left hanging:

> I like to be called a good man and someone who's wise. You already know that about me. . . . If a slave of mine comes to me and says, "I didn't run away or commit any robbery," I'm the kind of guy who would say, "Here's some good news for you. No need to worry about getting beat with a whip." And if the slave says, "I haven't killed anyone," then I'd say, "Good. We don't have to hang you on a cross and feed you to those scavenger crows."
>
> *Epistles*, 1.16 (20 BC)

In the poem, he used crucifixion as an example of overkill in a case when the punishment didn't fit the crime.

A FARMER WITH TIME TO WRITE POETRY

Quintus Horatius Flaccus, son of a former slave, fought for the wrong general in a Roman civil war. He fought for Brutus, who had helped assassinate Julius Caesar. When the battle turned against Brutus, Horace said he dropped his shield and ran in full retreat for his life.

He lost his job in the military for that. He lost his family estate, too. Winners of the war confiscated it and gave it to some of their retiring soldiers.

Yet years later the general who won the battle—and who became Emperor Augustus—asked Horace to write poetry for him.

Augustus pardoned the soldiers who fought against him, Horace among them. Horace moved to Rome and took a job as a clerk in the treasury.

He was about 23 years old, and smart—educated in the most respected school in Rome, the Grammar School of Orbilius. He had studied literature and philosophy in Athens, as well.

In Rome he made friends with poets Virgil and Varius. But perhaps his most important connection came when a famously rich advisor to Augustus took a liking to him: Gaius Cilnius Maecenas. That rich gentleman set him up for life by giving him or loaning him a farm near Tivoli, along a scenic mountain pass about 16 miles (25 km) east of Rome. Horace suddenly had free time to write poetry. That's probably courtesy of slave labor, historians speculate. If not, farmers today would like to know his trick for running a farm while finding time to write poetry. After a dawn-to-dusk day of driving a plow, a worn-out farmer typically won't curl up with a quill and a bowl of barley beer. (Well, maybe the beer.)

Horace is most famous for writing *Odes*, a collection of four books about a scattered mess of life's topics—often the ordinary stuff: love, wine, and friendship. He also criticized wrongs he saw in society, along with the arrogance and hypocrisy of the Roman Empire.

One letter Augustus reportedly wrote described Horace as short and exceedingly well fed. Horace at age 44 admitted to being short. He also acknowledged he was gray-haired and irritable.

QUINTUS HORATIUS FLACCUS, better known as Horace, was a Roman poet described in his day as short, well-fed, and irritable. This first-century Roman sculpture shows two men at a banquet.

CRUCIFIED FOR EATING LEFTOVERS?

Since we don't have any hope of wiping out awful vices such as anger, can't we at least use common sense when it comes time to punish people? Why can't the punishment weigh the same as the crime? That would make perfect sense.

Let's say a master orders his slave to clear the dinner table and that while the slave carries off the dishes, he gobbles down the leftover, half-eaten fish while it's still soaking in warm sauce. If his owner punishes him by sending him to the cross, people will think the guy has lost his mind. A person like that would be crazier than Labeo [a mystery person]. An irrational, barbaric crime like that would be far worse than what the slave did.

Satire, 1.3

CRUCIFIED BIRD FOOD

Poetry and crucifixion don't sound like they would go well together. But plenty of Roman poets wrote about it.

One of them was a man named Juvenal, born in AD 50, about the time Paul was wrapping up his last church-starting mission trip through Turkey and Greece.

Vultures soar from dead donkey to dead dog to whatever is left on the crosses.
Then back to the nest they fly, bringing their young a meal torn from cadavers and carcasses.

Satire, 14.77–78

BIRD WATCHING. Romans, it seems, often left crucified people hanging on the cross long after the victim died. Horace wrote that vultures feed their young from "whatever is left on the crosses . . . bringing their young a meal torn from cadavers."

BURIAL PORTRAIT of a Middle Eastern man from around AD 100, about the time Titus Flavius Josephus died. There's no surviving image of Josephus, who was born as Joseph, son of Matthias.

CHAPTER 4

"EVERY DAY, ROMAN SOLDIERS CAUGHT 500 JEWS OR MORE"

—JOSEPHUS
(ABOUT AD 37–100)

*Roman citizen, Jewish historian, and collaborator
who advised the invading Roman army as it
crushed a Jewish revolt, leveled Jerusalem, and
destroyed the world's only Jewish temple*

Josephus commanded a Jewish militia the Roman army quickly over-ran during the Jewish Revolt started in AD 66. Then he defected and became a collaborator. Suddenly, he found himself in the perfect spot to witness crucifixions.

After Roman General Vespasian and his son General Titus crushed the Jewish rebellion, Josephus became an eyewitness to hundreds, maybe thousands, of crucifixions of his Jewish countrymen.

His writings reveal a staggering brutality in the way Roman soldiers executed their defeated enemies. Here's an excerpt paraphrased into casual English:

> First, they were beaten. Then they were ridiculed. They were tortured in lots of different ways before they finally died, crucified outside Jerusalem's city walls. [Roman General] Titus actually

pitied them—very much. Every day Roman soldiers caught 500 Jews or more. Titus decided it wasn't safe to let them go. And he couldn't spare the soldiers it would take to guard that many prisoners.

Titus let his soldiers unload on the captives and treat them miserably. He did that because he hoped the horror of it might convince Jews inside the city to surrender. He hoped they realized that if they didn't surrender, they would get the same treatment.

Soldiers, driven by their hatred of the Jews, nailed them to crosses. They nailed them in many different positions to entertain themselves and to horrify the Jews watching this spectacle from inside the walled city of Jerusalem.

In time, soldiers ran out of wood for crosses. But it didn't matter because they had run out of room for crosses even if they had found more wood.

War of the Jews, 5.11.1

It's hard to tell whether Josephus felt any guilt for his treason, or any responsibility for the wholesale deaths of so many of his countrymen. And then there's the leveling of Jerusalem and the world's only Jew-

ish temple, which has never been rebuilt. Jews haven't rebuilt it because a 1,400-year-old Muslim shrine sits on the site: the Dome of the Rock, Jerusalem's most famous landmark today.

CREATIVE CRUCIFIXION. "Soldiers, driven by their hatred of the Jews, nailed them . . . in many different positions to entertain themselves." —Josephus.

JERUSALEM FALLS. Jews make their last stand at the temple altar in Jerusalem, as Romans overrun the temple and the entire city, eventually leveling both. Outside the city walls, Josephus said Romans crucified hundreds of Jews they'd captured during the four-month siege.

But Josephus made this much incredibly clear: crucifixion in Roman times was a horrible, degrading, unspeakable way to die.

THREE FRIENDS TAKEN OFF CROSSES ALIVE

Josephus managed to get three of his crucified friends taken down from their crosses and medically treated.

He got the permission from General Titus, commander of the Roman army that had crushed the Jewish revolt and leveled Jerusalem. Titus was that grateful for the help Josephus provided as a former Jewish soldier who switched sides and became a chief advisor for the Roman invaders.

Josephus said he spotted his friends hanging on crosses after a visit to Tekoa, a village about half a day's walk (12 miles or 20 km) south of Jerusalem.

> Caesar Titus sent me to the village of Tekoa with [General] Cerialis and his cavalry of a thousand men. We went there to see if it would be a good place to build a walled camp.

JOSEPHUS, JEWISH TRAITOR WHO WROTE JEWISH HISTORY

Titus Flavius Josephus was a Jew who probably didn't get many invitations to a circumcision.

It doesn't matter that he's the most famous Jewish historian this side of Moses and the primary source of eyewitness information about Romans in the first century and about the Jewish War of Independence against Rome (AD 66–73). His people blamed him for dooming their fight against the Romans—invaders who had occupied their homeland for a century. He's well-regarded by scholars nowadays, but his own people considered him a coward and a traitor.

He was 29 years old when Jewish elders launched a revolt against Rome and gave him command of a militia of Jews stationed in Galilee, on the northern front of the Jewish homeland.

Jews had revolted in AD 66, chasing out the few Roman soldiers posted there and then taking back their nation. Freedom lasted a few months, anyhow.

But the next spring, a Roman army of 60,000 soldiers invaded, led by their premier general, Vespasian, along with his son Titus. Roman armies swarmed into Galilee first. Josephus not only surrendered, he defected. But not before choreographing the suicide of most of his remaining men.

Romans had caught his militia holed up in the Galilean city of Jotapata. That was good news for the Roman army. Siege

TITUS

warfare was their specialty. Romans may have lost more men if Josephus had decided to hit and run, using guerrilla tactics that had helped Jews win their freedom from a Greek occupying force some 200 years earlier.

Josephus wrote that during the battle for Jotapata, he and the remnant of his militia—40 men—got trapped in a cave. Josephus wrote that the men decided to kill themselves rather than surrender. They made a suicide pact, agreeing to cut each other's throats. Josephus said it was his idea to draw lots, which was a bit like picking the short straw from a handful of straws. In this case, they may have used numbered or colored stones.

Josephus said he told his men, "Whoever draws the first lot gets killed by the man who draws the second lot. This way, the luck of the draw will work its way through all of us" (*War of the Jews*, 3.8.7).

Josephus said that the man whose number came up first "stretched out his neck for the man whose number came up second." One by one, a man cut the throat of a comrade and then died at the blade of another. In what many historians say was probably lot-tampering or sleight of hand, Josephus became the last man standing, along with one other militiaman.

They decided to die another day.

Josephus surrendered and joined the Romans as an advisor, translator, and go-between who tried talking other Jews into surrendering. He praised General Vespasian, correctly predicting that the general would become Rome's next emperor. It was a fair and educated guess because Romans often picked their emperors from among their best generals. In fact, a couple of years later, while Vespasian was still besieging Jerusalem in AD 69, the Roman Senate declared him the new emperor. The previous emperor, Nero, had killed himself.

Vespasian rewarded Josephus for his prediction and his services by adopting him as a son. Josephus won

- Roman citizenship;
- free housing in Rome, in a former palace of Vespasian;
- pension income for life; and
- the release of some of his friends, who had been taken captive.

Jews were not impressed.

During the siege of Jerusalem, Romans had asked Josephus to walk up to the wall and try talking some sense into the Jews. Romans had surrounded the city with dirt embankments and trenches. There was no safe way to sneak in or out of town. Jose-

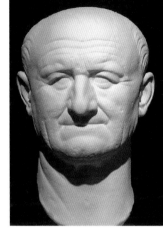

VESPASIAN

phus pleaded with the Jews to surrender.

Someone on the wall threw a rock at him, bopped him a good one on the head, and knocked him out. Jews inside celebrated because they thought they had killed the no-good defector. Romans rescued and revived him.

Jewish hatred of Josephus might help explain why not one shred of any of his original books has survived. And there were plenty of books.

- *Antiquities of the Jews*, 20 volumes of Jewish history, intended to help Romans appreciate Jews and their traditions
- *War of the Jews*, 7 volumes about the failed Jewish War of Independence
- *The Life of Flavius Josephus*, an autobiography that wouldn't make a good gift at a bar mitzvah
- *Against Apion*, two books of a debate in which Josephus defends the Jewish religion

Josephus is one of the most important go-to sources for historians who want to know what happened during his century—the century in which Jesus lived and was crucified, and when the Christian movement started.

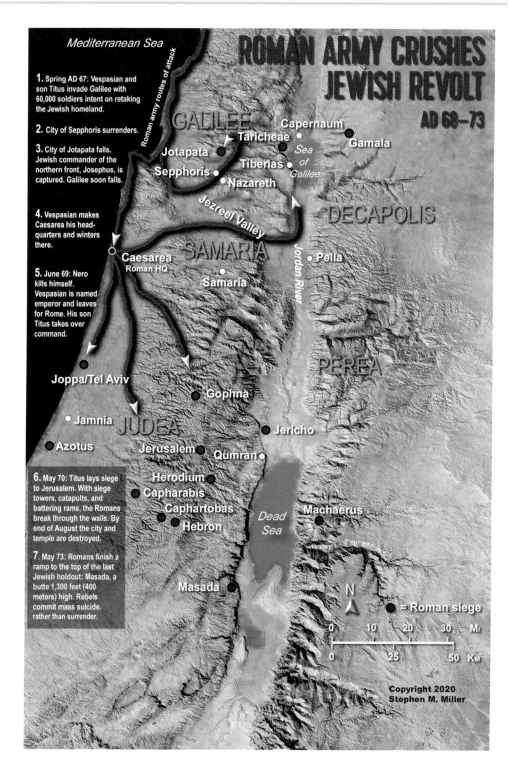

Mediterranean Sea

ROMAN ARMY CRUSHES JEWISH REVOLT

AD 68–73

1. Spring AD 67: Vespasian and son Titus invade Galilee with 60,000 soldiers intent on retaking the Jewish homeland.

2. City of Sepphoris surrenders.

3. City of Jotapata falls. Jewish commander of the northern front, Josephus, is captured. Galilee soon falls.

4. Vespasian makes Caesarea his head-quarters and winters there.

5. June 69: Nero kills himself. Vespasian is named emperor and leaves for Rome. His son Titus takes over command.

6. May 70: Titus lays siege to Jerusalem. With siege towers, catapults, and battering rams, the Romans break through the walls. By end of August the city and temple are destroyed.

7. May 73: Romans finish a ramp to the top of the last Jewish holdout: Masada, a butte 1,300 feet (400 meters) high. Rebels commit mass suicide. rather than surrender.

Roman army routes of attack

GALILEE

Capernaum

Taricheae

Gamala

Jotapata

Sea of Galilee

Sepphoris

Tiberias

Nazareth

DECAPOLIS

Jezreel Valley

Jordan River

SAMARIA

Pella

Caesarea
Roman HQ

Samaria

PEREA

Joppa/Tel Aviv

Gophna

Jamnia

JUDEA

Jericho

Azotus

Jerusalem

Qumran

Herodium

Capharabis

Caphartobas

Dead Sea

Machaerus

Hebron

Masada

N

▲ = Roman siege

0   10   20   30   Mɪ

0   25   50 Kм

Copyright 2020
Stephen M. Miller

On the trip back, I saw many prisoners crucified alongside the route. Among them were three people I recognized, my close colleagues.

I was overcome with grief. It crushed my soul. I went to Titus and told him about it, weeping as I spoke.

He didn't hesitate. Instantly he gave orders that my friends be taken down and given the best medical treatment.

I'm sad to say that two of them died during the treatment. But the third one lived.

Life of Josephus, 420–421

JEW CRUCIFIES 800 FELLOW JEWS

Two armies stood facing one another in the hills around Shechem, in what is now the heart of the Holy Land. Jews were about to fight on both sides of that battle. It was one of many battles before and after, in what became known as the Judean Civil War.

Alexander Jannaeus (about 103–76 BC), Jewish king of Judea, led the local army. Josephus reports that Alexander mustered a force of about 20,000 Jews and 6,200 mercenaries. Demetrius, king of Syria (96–87 BC), led the invasion force: 3,000 cavalrymen, 40,000 infantry.

As the armies squared off, Demetrius tried to convince mercenaries with Alexander to come and join him, since many of the mercenaries were Greek. And Alexander tried to convince Jews in Demetrius's army to come over and join him. No one flipped.

It's no surprise who won the battle of 26,200 versus 43,000. Math won. Alexander lost.

All of Alexander's mercenaries died, either in battle or by execution. Alexander escaped into the mountains. About 6,000 Jews who had fought with Demetrius began to feel sorry for their defeated king. So they flipped sides and joined him. That worried Demetrius. So, he retreated to his capital in Damascus.

Some Jews still opposed Alexander, and they fought the remnant of his army. Alexander's forces slaughtered them and captured about 800 of the leaders.

MASS EXECUTION. Jewish regional king, Alexander Jannaeus, enjoys a banquet while giving the order to execute 800 fellow Jews and their families, mainly Pharisees. The executed Jews had joined a rebel army fighting against the king, but they lost the war.

Alexander brought the captives to Jerusalem. There, he did one of the most barbaric things one human could do to another. While he was throwing a party and eating with the concubines in his harem, he gave the order. Crucifixion. With the entire city gathered to watch, he ordered the crucifixion of about 800 men.

Before they died, he ordered their families brought out where they could see them. Then he ordered his men to cut the throats of all those women and children. He did this out of revenge for what they had done to hurt him. Still, this punishment was absolutely inhumane.

Antiquities of the Jews, 13.14

CRUCIFIED FOR REFUSING TO QUIT THE JEWISH FAITH

Jews couldn't be Jews when Antiochus IV Epiphanes (about 215–164 BC) ruled their corner of the Middle East, from his capital in Syria. He outlawed the Jewish religion.

That was a switch. His father, Antiochus III the Great, hadn't been like that at all.

But Epiphanes apparently worked himself into a mood. He was on his way home from almost conquering Egypt. A Roman ambassador intercepted him when he was about to finish the war and told him if he didn't turn around and go home, the Roman Empire would declare war on him. So he went home, bummed.

He made a stop in Jerusalem.

He said he came in peace, so the Jews let him in. That was a mistake. He looted the city, including the world's only Jewish temple. He took the temple's golden candlesticks, the golden incense altar, the table that held the sacred bread, and even the curtains that cordoned off the most sacred room, the Holy of Holies.

ANTIOCHUS IV EPIPHANES
on coin he minted.

Then he decided to take the Jewishness out of the Jewish homeland. He was going to make it Greek in both culture and religion.

The king turned the temple altar of God into an altar for idols—the gallery of Roman gods. Then he sacrificed a pig. Roman gods loved pork, but it was ritually unclean to the Jews—not kosher. If there is such a thing as an abomination, it would be sacrificing a pig on the altar in the Jewish temple at Jerusalem.

> He ordered the Jews to stop worshiping God. From now on they were to worship his gods [especially Zeus].
>
> He ordered them to build temples to those gods. And in every city and village they needed a sacrificial altar. There, they were supposed to sacrifice a pig a day.
>
> He told the Jews to stop circumcising their baby sons, and he threatened to punish them if they broke any of his laws.
>
> He appointed minders to keep an eye on the behavior of people and to force them to do as they were told.
>
> Many Jews did just that. Some had no problem doing it. Others did it only because they were afraid of getting punished.

CRUCIFIED WOMEN. Antiochus IV Epiphanes not only crucified Jewish women for practicing their faith, a religion he outlawed; if they got caught with a circumcised baby, he strangled both. Then he hung the baby around the dead mother's neck and crucified their corpses.

But the best of the people ignored the king's orders. Those were the people with the strongest spirit. They were more devoted to their people's traditions than they were afraid of the king's punishment.

They paid a high price every day. They were made miserable with torture. They were beaten with rods. Their bodies were pulled apart limb by limb. Some were crucified while they were still alive and breathing.

The king ordered his people to strangle the little boys who were circumcised and to strangle their mothers as well. Then he had the dead baby boys tied around the necks of their dead mothers. Together, they were hung on crosses.

Antiquities of the Jews, 12.256

Jews soon rebelled, launching what became known as the Maccabean Revolt (167–160 BC), which the Jews won. They remained free for a century, until General Pompey of Rome arrived and turned the Jewish homeland into a satellite kingdom of Rome.

PRIESTS CRUCIFIED FOR COLLUDING WITH ADULTERER

In Rome's caste system—the levels of status in society—Decius Mundus was a rich, upper crust Roman of the equestrian class, one notch below the top-dog senatorial class. He seemed to think this entitled him to have sex with a married woman named Paulina.

She wanted nothing to do with him. She was beautiful, rich, and highly respected for her modesty.

Apparently not the romantic, Mundus offered her money for a one-night stand. What he lacked in warm-hearted sweet nothings, he made up for in cold currency. The offer was almost a ton of silver, 200,000 drachma. Holy moly, that's a lot of money.

Sadly for him, she didn't need the coins.

Apparently, he decided to kill himself.

Curiously, he started spreading the word.

The daughter of a slave his father had freed—a creatively mischievous woman named Ide—told him she could help him land the lady. For a small fee of 50,000 drachma. That's a savings of 150,000 drachma.

Ide realized she couldn't buy Paulina. But she learned that Paulina was devoted to the gods, and especially to Isis. So Ide went to the Isis temple and bribed the priests into figuring out a way to help this man achieve the object of his lust.

The leading priests met privately with Paulina and told her that Anubis, the protector of Isis, wanted to spend the night

ISIS PRIESTS CRUCIFIED. Bust of an Isis priest, found in Italy and dated to the first century BC. Emperor Tiberias crucified some Isis priests and demolished the temple after they tricked an attractive Isis worshiper into having sex with one of the men in town. She thought she was having sex with a god.

with her. Paulina met with her husband and the two decided that this was a perfectly acceptable way of expressing their worship.

Paulina was served supper at the temple and then ushered into the temple's most sacred room. Priests shut the door behind her. When Mundus appeared in the darkness, Paulina had no idea it was him.

Afterward, she told her friends she had spent the night with Anubis. Josephus, in telling the story, implies there were some eyes rolling:

> Three days after the event, Mundus met Paulina.
>
> He said, "Well, Paulina, you saved me a ton of silver. That's money you could have added to your family treasure. But I'd like you to know that you provided the service I requested anyhow. As for all those times you turned me down, no big deal. I got what I wanted and I'm happy I did. I had to borrow the name of Anubis, though."
>
> Then he left.
>
> When Paulina realized what she had done, she felt sick. She ripped her clothes and told her husband the vile and twisted story of what this man had done to her. She begged her husband to do something about it.
>
> He took the matter up with Emperor Tiberius. The emperor conducted a thorough investigation. After interrogating the priests, he ordered them crucified. Ditto for Ide who caused all this trouble by conceiving the plan that so terribly injured Paulina.
>
> Tiberius also ordered the temple of Isis demolished and her statue thrown into the Tiber River.
>
> As for Mundus, Tiberius did nothing more than banish him. The emperor figured this was a crime of love and that Mundus had simply let his passions get the better of him.
>
> *Antiquities of the Jews,* 18.3

CHAPTER 5

"THE CROSS ... IT'S MY FAMILY TOMB"

—PLAUTUS (ABOUT 254–184 BC)

Roman playwright of comedies that are among the oldest surviving literary works written in Latin, the native language of the Roman Empire

Curses and comedy, that's where crucifixion first shows up in ancient Roman writing.

More than 200 years before Romans crucified Jesus, a Roman comic writer named Plautus was writing Greek-style theater plays in Latin, the language of the Roman Empire. Like writers of movies, monologues, and memes today, he used comedy to wage an assault on serious wrongs in the world.

One play, *Captives*, spins its storyline around innocent people captured as prisoners of war and then sold into slavery.

MOSAIC OF ACTORS IN POMPEII, ITALY. Plautus's actors may have worn costumes like this to help represent different characters in the comedies he wrote.

Comic relief comes from a character named Ergasilus. Look up the word and we find it's a crustacean called "gill lice." Ergasilus is a parasite. It latches onto the gills of fish and then feeds off the fish's blood and soft tissue in the gills. That's pretty much what the comic character does. He mooches off other people for free food and housing. He calls himself a parasite, and he calls his profession the parasitic art. In one scene Ergasilus is hungry. Complaining about his business of mooching off others, Ergasilus is cussing mad and he invokes the Latin word *crux*, for cross. It's one of the oldest mentions of the cross in Roman writings.

> To hell on the damned cross with this parasitic art—this business
> of sucking up to people so they'll give us some food.
>
> *Captives*, act 3, scene 1

"TAKE HER . . . "

In the play *Casina*, Plautus creates the character of a dirty old man named Stalino who plots to spend some nonconsensual quality time with a beautiful young woman who is not his wife. The lust of his life who's not his wife is Casina.

Stalino talks his reluctant neighbor into letting him use his home as a temporary love nest. And he talks his wife into inviting the neighbor's

THE CHRISTIAN LEGACY

Some strong words and bawdy scenes in this chapter may leave folks feeling uncomfortable. We include them because they are the first Roman words on record that mention crucifixion.

These words add to the weight of shame connected to the cross. Off-color stories and profanity are what Romans associated with crucifixion.

It's as though it wasn't enough to in-terrogate Jesus, torture him, beat him, strip him, and execute him. He had to be killed in the most humiliating way known to man.

These words of Plautus are part of our legacy as Christians. These are words we should remember when we think about the sacrifice of Jesus—it is right for us to feel the embarrassment and the shame of them.

wife to stay with her and help prepare for a wedding party—to get her out of the neighbor's house he wants to use.

When the neighbor's wife doesn't show up on time, Stalino goes over to the neighbor and reminds him of the agreement. The angry neighbor uses the Latin *crucem*, a form of *crux* for cross, to cuss the old lecher out while grudgingly agreeing to send his wife over to get her out of the house:

> Go ahead and take her [my wife] all the way to hell on a cross. Take her and your wife and your secret lover, too. I'll tell my wife right now to head on over through the garden to your wife.
>
> *Casina*, act 3, scene 4

"I'LL BE BURIED ON THE CROSS"

A slave in Plautus's comedy *The Braggart Soldier* hints at how common it was for Roman slave masters to crucify their disobedient slaves. It also hints that it was common for Romans to leave the bodies decaying on the cross. No burial, at least in some cases.

As the story goes, a soldier from Ephesus, on what is now Turkey's west coast, kidnaps a lady of the

WHAT'S YOUR BID? A Roman auctioneer takes bids on a slave. In Plautus's comedy, *The Braggart Soldier*, one slave threatens another with crucifixion. The threatened says he already knows the cross will be his grave, just as it was for his fathers. "It's the family tomb."

PLAUTUS, THE COMEDIAN

Titus Maccius Plautus, from a small town in northern Italy, put a Roman face on comedy.

That was new. Romans had watched tragedies, comedies, and adventures from various Roman playwrights, but it was all Greek to them. The setting of plays had always been Greece. That's because the stories were Greek. Roman writers merely recycled classic Greek stories and dialogue.

Plautus started changing that. He switched the setting. He wrote Rome into the stories. He talked about Roman towns, streets, gates, laws, and businesses. They all became targets or tools for him to use to critique the world while entertaining an audience—a bit like some comedians do today.

He started tweaking and rewriting the Greek plots and scenes, adding a pun here and slapstick joke there. He left his creative ink stains on an estimated 130 plays, though only twenty have survived as copies of the original. There are fragments of about thirty other plays, as well.

He became so popular that other writers put his name on their plays to lure in a bigger audience. The opposite of plagiarism. But the definition of marketing. And of lying.

These comedies—oddly enough—preserve some of the oldest known references to crucifixion.

---

night in Athens. The woman's name is Philo. The soldier takes her by force to live with him.

Philo's true love tracks her down and quickly gets reacquainted with her, so to speak.

While the two are reacquainting, the soldier's slave, Sceledra, happens to see them.

Uh-oh.

Well, the woman's true love has a smart slave of his own, Palaestrio. The soldier's slave, on the other hand, isn't a candidate for philosophy classes in Athens. So Palaestrio (smart slave) and Philo (kidnapped woman) decide to convince Sceledra (not-so-smart slave) into believing he didn't see what he insists he saw, "By god, I did." (The god he invoked was Hercules, but "by Hercules" no longer expresses the tone he intended. So, the paraphrase.)

As Sceledra sits with his arms stretched out, Palaestrio walks up to him and begins trying to reprogram his memory, first with intimidation. The cross comes up twice during the exchange:

PALAESTRIO: [To Sceledra, who's resting with arms outstretched.] "Know what? I think you're going to look just like this very soon, when they march you out the city gates. Yep, your arms are going to stretch out on a cross you'll have to carry."

SCELEDRA: "You don't say. For what?"

PALAESTRIO: "Look left. Do you know what that woman is?"

SCELEDRA: "Yes I do, by god. That girl is the master's lover. . . ."

PHILO: "You troublemaker. You said you saw me kissing someone in the neighbor's house?"

SCELEDRA: "By god, I did."

PHILO: "Me? You saw me?"

SCELEDRA: "With these two eyeballs, by god."

PHILO: "You'll lose them soon. They're seeing things. . . ."

SCELEDRA: "You can stop threatening me anytime now. I already know I'll be buried on the cross. That's where they buried everyone in my family. My father. My grandfather. My great-grandfather. My great-great-grandfather. And my great-great-great-grandfather. It's the family tomb."

The Braggart Soldier, act 2, scene 8

UNKNOWN MAN FROM FIRST CENTURY.
There are no known images of Pliny, but the man sculpted here lived at about the same time he did—during the first century, when the disciples of Jesus were starting the Christian movement.

CHAPTER 6

RX FOR FEVER: "TAKE A PIECE OF NAIL OFF OF A CROSS"

PLINY THE ELDER (AD 23–79)

Roman writer who wrote Natural History, *an encyclopedia-style, 37-volume series of books about topics such as plants, animals, farming, and medical treatments*

Pliny is the go-to source for anyone who wants to know what health-care was like in the time of Jesus. Pliny's 37-volume encyclopedia set called *Natural History* includes five books on healthcare. Those books feature lists of remedies he came across during his research.

This is especially intriguing because he was alive when Jesus and the disciples were practicing medicine by healing the sick.

Among Pliny's collected healthcare remedies:

- *Some seem bizarre.* Sore joints: Body oil and sweat scraped from an athlete. Apply topically. Available for purchase from gymnasium owners (*Natural History* 28.13).

- *Some sound a little like techniques Jesus used* (John 9:6–7). Prevent eye disease: Every day, touch your eyes three times with the muddy water you get when you wash your feet (*Natural History* 28.10).

MOUNT VESUVIUS WAS NOT KIND TO PLINY

Gaius Plinius Secundus, better known as Pliny the Elder, was a science writer fascinated with the natural world and everything in it. The natural world killed him.

He died in the eruption of Mount Vesuvius, while commanding the Roman fleet that patrolled the Bay of Naples at the foot of the volcano.

Pliny went ashore to rescue some friends. But a roiling cloud of volcanic ash sucked the oxygen out of the air and darkened the sky for three days. Pliny suffocated to death. An estimated 16,000 souls or more died in this disaster that destroyed the cities of Pompeii and Herculaneum.

Born into a rich family, Pliny became a soldier at age 23. He rose to the rank of cavalry commander and served in what is now Germany with General Vespasian, Rome's future emperor.

Pliny went into semiretirement in Rome and started writing. His most famous project was an encyclopedia of natural science, thirty-seven volumes in a series called *Natural History*. He wrote in detail about diseases and medical treatments for sickness and in-

DEATH MOLD. Ash from erupting Mt. Vesuvius created casts of people in Pompeii as they died.

juries. He also wrote about plants, animals, and geography.

What readers found especially helpful was that he organized his observations into categories. He would pick a disease and then report a long list of treatments that people used to treat that disease. That

- *Some seem to back up what Bible writers reported.* Consider the case of the woman with heavy menstrual bleeding (Mark 5:25–34). She spent all her savings on trying to find a cure. Pliny lists scores of treatments for that problem— enough to bankrupt a family. One treatment: Crush several snails. Mix them with starch and the sap of the locoweed or the goat's thorn plant. Apply topically as a liniment (*Natural History* 30.43).

made it easier to pick up on similarities and links among the sicknesses and the treatments.

When Pliny's army buddy Vespasian became emperor, Pliny came out of semi-retirement and took on several assignments. His last job was to command the fleet off the coast of Naples, protecting ships and people along the coastline from pirates.

Pliny's nephew, Pliny the Younger, wrote the story of the eruption and the death of his uncle. Younger Pliny watched the eruption from the safety of Elder Pliny's home in Misenum, now Miseno, a city 20 miles (32 km) across the bay.

GOODBYE POMPEII. Mt. Vesuvius erupts in AD 79, shrouding Pompeii and neighboring towns in fiery ash that killed thousands, including Pliny, a fleet commander who came ashore on a mission to rescue friends.

Crucified people provided resources, too, Pliny reported. In book 28 of his series, he devoted two chapters to remedies that require something from the dead. He said that some objects used in crucifixion can be helpful in treating what he called quartan fever. That's a fever that recurs about every three or four days, like malaria.

Here's how to treat recurring fever. Take a piece of nail off a cross. As an alternative, take a piece of rope that someone used in

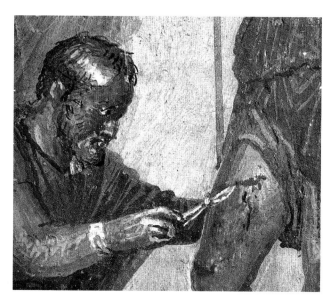

WOUNDED WARRIOR. A physician removes an arrowhead from a warrior's leg. Pliny reported on medical treatments and medicines used by physicians during the century Jesus lived. Two of his 37 volumes of *Natural History* deal with the practice of medicine and magic. Some medical treatments called for nails from a crucifixion.

crucifixion. Wrap either one of these in wool and tie it to the patient's neck. Pay attention to this instruction: The moment the patient recovers, take the wool and its contents away and hide them in a hole where the sunlight can't reach them.

Natural History, 28.11

AFRICANS CRUCIFY MAN-EATING LIONS

Pliny says people weren't the only ones crucified. So were lions and dogs. Drawing on the writings of an earlier Greek historian, Polybius (about 200–118 BC), Pliny said Carthaginians (in what is now an African city on the northern coast of Libya) crucified lions who had grown so hungry that they started approaching populated areas and attacking people.

> Polybius . . . saw that when African lions got too old to hunt wild animals they waited outside cities and attacked humans. He said he and Scipio [about 236–183 BC; Roman general famous for defeating Hannibal of Carthage] saw that Africans in those cities responded by crucifying lions on a cross. People said that when other lions saw this, they would stop the outrageous attacks out of the fear that they could face the same punishment.
>
> *Natural History,* 8.18

"DOGS WERE CRUCIFIED ALIVE"

Rome was under attack from invaders. Six of the seven hills that made up Rome had already fallen. The last fortress standing was on Capitoline Hill. During a lull in the fighting, in the deep black of night, guard dogs failed to alert the Romans that a stealth attack had started, that the enemy had arrived and was climbing up the hillside cliffs.

Because the dogs slept, dogs to come would pay the price in a macabre yearly ritual.

Roman guards also missed the sound of the approaching soldiers. We can guess what happened to them.

Sacred geese in Jupiter's temple were the heroes. They heard the invaders. These geese became the first alert. They honked so loudly they woke up the Roman army that had retreated onto the hilltop fortress.

Romans pushed the invaders off the cliff.

Each year afterward on August 3, Romans honored the sacred geese in a ritual called Dog Punishment. That's *supplicia canum* in their native Latin.

Romans paraded a lucky goose through the town on a decorated litter. A dog was in the parade, too.

BAD DOG. An artist chiseled this sculpture into white marble during Roman times, somewhere between the 100s BC and the AD 300s. Once a year, Romans crucified dogs for something that some of their ancestors failed to do.

> Every year, dogs were crucified alive on a cross or a stake made of elder wood. They were paraded between the temple of Juventas [Roman goddess of protection and of children] and the temple of Summanus [god of nighttime thunder].
>
> *Natural History*, 29.14; and Plutarch's
> *On the Fortune of the Romans*, 12

FUNERAL PORTRAIT OF A ROMAN MAN
who lived around the AD 100s, the time of
novelist Apuleius.

CHAPTER 7

"FIXINGS OF WITCHCRAFT ... FLESH STILL STUCK TO THE NAILS"

—APULEIUS
(ABOUT AD 124–170)

Roman author of Metamorphoses, *the only surviving ancient Roman novel written in Rome's native language of Latin*

Lucius, a character in a Roman novel, gets obsessively curious about the magic arts. After he watches a witch turn herself into a bird, he decides to give it a try and morph himself into a bird, too.

That might be why author Apuleius called the story *Metamorphoses*.

Lucius goofs up the magical spell, however, and turns himself into a donkey.

That might have something to do with why most people today call the book by its nickname: *The Golden Ass*.

On the first night after the metamorphosis, Lucius's girlfriend parks him in a barn. Sadly, mule thieves steal him before dawn. The novel, spanning eleven books, is the adventurous story of this man's four-footed travels and—spoiler alert—his return to human form at the end of the journey.

WITCHCRAFT RX. Crucifixion nails showed up on the shopping list of witches and priestesses of sorcery. So said Roman novelist Apuleius, along with Roman natural history writer Pliny, among others. Sorcery aficionados and their cult members reportedly used the nails along with crucifixion body parts in their magic and spells. Circe, goddess of sorcery portrayed here, reportedly inspired cults that practiced dark magic and talking with spirits of the dead. Emperor Augustus burned books containing recipes for magical spells.

GNAWING FLESH OFF CRUCIFIXION NAILS

Roman poet Marcus Annaeus Lucanus (AD 39–65) penned a grizzly scene about a witch from Thessalonica, a city in what is now Greece, scavenging for supplies she could use in casting her spells.

> Corpses lie in stone tombs that absorb the body's moisture,
> with its filth inside the intestines, and all juices of the bone marrow.
> Then is when the witch swoops down like a starving vulture attacking limbs.
> She buries her hands in the eye sockets, scooping out the dry balls.
> From the crucified corpse she gnaws free the nails still stuck into the shrunken hands.
> She chews free the deadly ropes and knots that were used to help hang the body.
> She scrapes the crosses clean, taking everything human.
>
> *Civil War*, 6

But it all starts with Lucius visiting the home of a man whose wife practices witchcraft.

The list of ingredients she uses to whip up a spell is similar to ingredients that first-century science writer Pliny said that doctors used to treat the sick (see pages 77–80). One common ingredient for witch and doctor alike: a nail used in a crucifixion.

Here's how author Apuleius describes the witch's inventory of witchware:

> She set out all the usual fixings of witchcraft in her little laboratory of the damned. There were various drugs that pack a powerful smell. There were metal plates engraved with strange characters. And there were parts of birds associated with bad luck. There were human body parts as well, from the dead and from the buried: noses, fingers, and flesh still stuck to the nails from a cross.
>
> *Metamorphoses*, 3.17

SKETCH OF PLUTARCH based on a sculpture honoring him in his Greek hometown of Chaeronea, a three-day walk north of Corinth.

CHAPTER 8

"EACH CRIMINAL ... HAS TO CARRY HIS OWN CROSS"

—PLUTARCH
(ABOUT AD 45–125)

Greek author, known for his essays and his biographies of famous people

Why do the gods bother punishing people at all? They punish people too late for it to do any good. There's no deterrent in punishment that comes after the crime. Bad guys keep doing bad things.

That's pretty much the complaint Plutarch tackles in his essay sometimes called "On Delays of Divine Justice." This is just one of seventy-eight essays in a collection called *Morals* (*Moralia*).

In another essay, he mentions crucifixion. He says condemned criminals have to carry their own cross.

It's just a fleeting illustration he uses to make a point about why people seem to get away with sin and why the gods seem to delay punishment. But the reference seems to back up what the Bible says about Jesus carrying his cross (or a part of it):

> When we do something wrong, it takes a while for the punishment to catch up to us. That's generally what people say. That's what Plato said—we do something wrong and then comes the

CROSS OF SIN. "Each criminal condemned to crucifixion has to carry his own cross on his back," Plutarch wrote. "That's how it is for us when we do something wrong. In that moment we have to begin carrying the weight of the evil we've done." One of the Bible writers, however, wrote that Jesus carried our cross of sin. "Christ carried our sins in his body on the cross so we would stop living for sin and start living for what is right" (1 Peter 2:24 NCV).

punishment followed by the suffering, in that order. But I think we should listen instead to Hesiod [Greek poet in the 600s BC]. He said sin and the suffering it produces are twins, born at the same time. . . .

I've heard that the Spanish fly [one of the blister beetles], oddly enough, carries inside its body an antidote—a cure for the blisters it inflicts on people. [Active ingredient: cantharidin, a lethal poison used to treat warts and other skin bumps.] But that's exactly the opposite of how guilt works. When we do something wrong, guilt is right there with us, already producing punishment and pain.

Each criminal condemned to crucifixion has to carry his own cross on his back. That's how it is for us when we do something wrong. In that moment we have to begin carrying the weight of the evil we've done. The sin we've committed produces a terrible life for us—a life full of fear, painful emotions, endless regret, and high anxiety. . . .

PLUTARCH: I DON'T WRITE HISTORIES. I WRITE LIVES.

Six-year-old Plutarch was growing up in the Greek town of Chaeronea while the apostle Paul was starting a church in Corinth some 60 miles (100 km) south.

Like Paul, Plutarch was a Roman citizen who wrote a lot. But while Paul wrote letters, Plutarch later wrote essays and biographies. More than 200 of them, as far as history scholars can tell. His two most famous: *Parallel Lives,* about famous leaders, and *Moralia*, a series of 60 essays on ethics, religion, politics, and other topics.

While serving as a city leader in his hometown and running a school there, he did more than just write. He developed a style of writing that turned a corner on the typical biography of the day. Biographies back then didn't go very far into the character of a person.

He explained his approach to writing at the beginning of his story about Alexander the Great.

I don't plan to write about histories. I'm going to write about lives. A man's most celebrated accomplishments don't always tell us much about how good or bad he is. Sometimes we can learn more about a person's character and beliefs in a fleeting moment, an expression, or a laugh than we can learn by studying a famous siege they commanded, or impressive weaponry they amassed, or the bloodiest battles they fought.

Portrait artists pay more attention to the tiniest lines and features on a person's face than they do to the rest of the body. The face is where we find a person's character. So when I'm painting the life of a person with my words, I have to be allowed to look for the tiniest signs and slightest hints that reveal the soul. As for bigger stories and great battles, I'll leave those for other writers to explore.

Life of Alexander

MACEDONIA
Philippi
Thessalonica
Amphipolis
Apollonia
Berea

Aegean Sea

GREECE

ACHAIA
Chaeronea
hometown of Plutarch

Gulf of Corinth
Athens

Corinth

Many terribly sinful people seem to have a wonderful life. They're surrounded by a large family. They have important jobs in the community with lots of authority. It doesn't look like they're suffering for their sins until they get caught and executed or pushed off a cliff. We shouldn't call that punishment. It's only the end of the punishment.

On the Delays of Divine Vengeance
(De Sera Numinis Vindicta), 9.554

CRUCIFIED FOR EATING CHAMPION QUAIL

Quail fighting, popular in Roman times, is still popular in some parts of the world, especially in some Middle Eastern countries. The sport—advocates call it that—is not nearly as vicious as dogfighting or cockfighting, though the quail may not appreciate the distinction.

Pecking, clawing, and hopping around with tiny wings flailing usu-

CRUCIFIED ON A SHIP'S MAST. With Rome's naval Battle of Actium won and Egypt's Queen Cleopatra dead, General Augustus got a complaint. One of Egypt's governors bought and ate the champion fighting quail. Augustus, soon to become emperor of Rome, ordered that champion-quail-eating governor nailed to a ship's mast.

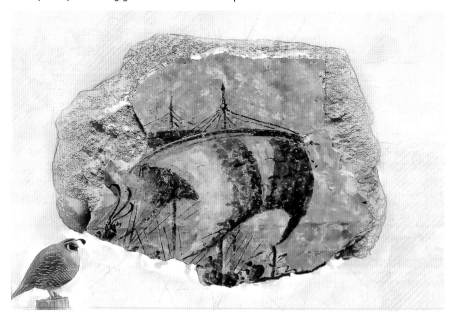

ally lasts just two or three minutes—at least in the modern version of quail fighting, which are available to see in videos online. The fight ends when one bird walks away.

People today bet on the bird they think will win. It's a fair bet that folks also wagered on the quail fights 2,000 years ago.

One Roman emperor, Marcus Aurelius Antonius (AD 121–180), wrote about quail fighting in a book called *Meditations*. He said that one of his tutors, Diognetus, taught him "not to breed quail for fighting, and not to obsess over the sport."

A century earlier, Augustus (aka Emperor Octavian) showed a fair amount of respect for champion quail—more respect than he had for an Egyptian governor.

Augustus had just won the battle of Actium, defeating the combined navies of his rival, Marc Antony, along with Egypt's Queen Cleopatra. Antony and Cleopatra committed suicide, and Augustus captured and spared the coastal city of Alexandria.

While Augustus was still there, someone told him that one of the governors in Egypt had been unkind to a champion quail.

> Augustus found out that Eros, a governor in Egypt, bought a champion quail. This quail beat every quail it ever fought. It was the undisputed [featherweight] champion quail.
>
> Eros roasted the bird and ate it.
>
> Augustus sent for Eros and asked him if it was true. Did he eat the champion quail?
>
> Eros admitted it.
>
> Augustus crucified him—nailed him to a ship's mast.
>
> *Sayings of the Romans*, "Caesar Augustus"

CHAIN GANG. In a scene preserved in marble from the AD 200s, a Roman soldier leads slaves to whatever comes next. In Chariton's novel, *Chaereas and Callirhoe*, 16 men chained together carry crosses to their crucifixion.

CHAPTER 9

"SIXTEEN MEN CHAINED TOGETHER"

—CHARITON
(ABOUT 25 BC–AD 50)

Greek novelist and author of Chaereas and Callirhoe, *a romance written perhaps just a decade or two after the crucifixion of Jesus*

*C*haereas and Callirhoe is a history-tied romance novel with a kickstart that's anything but romantic. The adventures begin after husband Chaereas kicks his pregnant wife, Callirhoe, into last Tuesday—hard enough to put her in a coma. Everyone thinks she's dead, so they bury her in a tomb with her family treasures. She doesn't stay put.

Her supernatural good looks are what got her there. As a character in a superhero movie, Callirhoe would simply walk around like a human stun gun, paralyzing people with her Aphrodite good looks.

Suitors in lust with her didn't care that she was married. They wanted her person. When no one could get it, the suitors joined forces to convince Callirhoe's husband that she had done the forbidden deed.

He believed the bad guys.

Lying on death's door in the tomb, Callirhoe wakes just in time to scare the goosebumps out of grave-robbing pirates. They get over the shock, however. And they steal her, too. They take her as a slave to Miletus, a city near Ephesus in what is now the west coast of Turkey.

This woman is so good looking that her slave owner marries her. She doesn't tell him that she's already married and pregnant.

Her first husband finds out she's alive. Chaereas goes after her, but gets himself enslaved, too.

In that setting, with Chaereas chained to 16 men about to attempt an escape, the story turns to the crucifixion of slaves:

> Sixteen men chained together in a little jail cell broke out of
> their chains at night. They managed to cut the guard's throat and

CRUCIFIED AND RELEASED—HERODOTUS (ABOUT 484–425 BC)

Known as "the Father of History," Herodotus is often considered the first historian to systematically collect information and analyze the supposed facts. He wrote *The Histories*, nine volumes about wars between Greeks and Persians.

Greek King Leonidas from the city of Sparta managed to hold off a Persian invasion force estimated at 100,000 men or more. Herodotus put the count at 241,400. Leonidas held the Persians for a week at the narrow pass of Thermopylae, though he commanded just 300 Spartan warriors and 700 militiamen from the Greek city of Thespiae.

One of history's most famous last stands, the story is captured with creativity and exaggeration in the blockbuster film *300*.

While the Spartans stood their ground, the Greek and Persian navies fought a sea battle at Artemisium (480 BC), north of Athens. Late to the battle was a formerly crucified Persian captain who lived to tell about it.

Fifteen Persian ships got a late start on the invasion of Greece. They put out to sea a long time after the escape. They didn't get very far because dogs started barking, sounding the alert. After they were caught, they were locked into wooden stocks for the night.

The next morning, the property manager told his boss, Governor Mithridates, what happened. The governor didn't bother to investigate the matter by meeting with the prisoners or hearing what they had to say. He ordered all sixteen men crucified.

The men were paraded out, chained together by the foot and

armada. When they finally reached the area of Artemisium, they caught sight of some Greek ships. They thought the Greek ships were part of their own fleet, and they made the mistake of sailing right into the waiting arms of their enemies.

The Persian commander was the viceroy who governed Cyme in Aeolia [a region on what is now Turkey's west coast]. His name was Sandoces and his father was Thamasius.

He had formerly served as one of the king's judges. King Darius arrested him and had him crucified for taking a bribe. But while Sandoces was still hanging on the cross and still alive, Darius had second thoughts. He concluded that the good in this man outweighed the bad. So the king decided he had acted too hastily, and he set Sandoces free.

Sandoces escaped with his life. But now he sailed right into the middle of a fleet of Greek ships. He didn't get lucky this time. When the Greeks saw the Persians sailing at them, they quickly figured out the Persians had made a big mistake. The Greeks put out to sea and easily captured the Persian ships.

SPARTAN WARRIOR

The Histories, 7.194.13

neck, each carrying his own cross. Executioners added this grim public spectacle to the punishment as an extra deterrent to any slaves thinking about committing the same crime.

Chaereas and Callirhoe, 4.2

More than just a romantic novel, it is one of the few that writes authentic history into the story. It's set about 400 years before Christ and it begins in Syracuse, a city on the island of Sicily, off the southern coast of Italy.

CITY THAT PRIVATIZED CRUCIFIXION

One company of undertakers in an ancient Roman town near Naples owned all the rights to make a living off the dying. They alone crucified criminals and buried nobles.

Cities today work out similar deals when they contract with one company to haul away the city's trash.

Two thousand years ago the city that privatized executions and funerals was known as Puteoli, home to an estimated 60,000 people. Today it's called Pozzuoli, located along Italy's west coast, about 150 miles (240 km) south of Rome (see map on page 47).

The contract that the city established with the undertaking company was important enough that they chiseled it into stone for the public to see. It turned up during World War II and is now on display in the Naples museum. The contract seems to date to sometime between 27 and 14 BC, about the time Mary the mother of Jesus would have been a child.

UNDERTAKER: MINIMUM REQUIREMENTS

Puteoli's contract says the undertaking company needed to employ at least 32 workers between the ages of 20 and 50.

City officials also said they didn't want to see anyone conducting an execution or a funeral who was

- bowlegged,
- crippled,
- tattooed,
- one-eyed, or, worse,
- blind in both eyes.

Scholars debate how to translate parts of the contract, since some words and letters are missing and the meaning of some words isn't clear.

Here's an attempt at paraphrasing two excerpts of the contract.

Privately funded crucifixion

When someone wants to hire the contractor to crucify one of his

The story wraps up with husband Chaereas getting free, joining the Egyptian rebellion against the Assyrian Empire, and winning a battle against the Persian army of Artaxerxes in Tyre, in what is now Lebanon. In case you're wondering, he rescues his wife from Persians who had taken her. Callirhoe happily sails home to Syracuse with her husband. Her slave master-husband keeps the child, whom he thinks is his. Callirhoe writes and tells him to raise the boy and then send him to her in Syracuse when he's grown.

---

slaves, the contractor must provide the wooden posts along with everything else that is necessary, including chains, cords for beating, and the workers who will administer the beating.

The person hiring the contractor will pay a day's wage [four sesterces, which equals one denarius] to each worker: those who carry the posts, administer the beating, and perform the execution.

Lex Puteoli, 2.8

Publicly funded crucifixion

When a city manager orders someone punished on behalf of the public, the contractor will provide this service at no cost. The contractor will set up the crosses and provide all the supplies at no charge, including nails, tar, wax, candles, and anything else required.

If the contractor is ordered to drag the body away using a hook, the people doing the work will dress in red clothes and ring a bell as they drag the body along.

Lex Puteoli, 2.11

It's unclear how the executioners used some of the supplies. Some scholars guess that the nails were to nail the person to the cross. As for the wax and candles, no one seems to think that's a courtesy for relatives on a night vigil with the body. Speculation is that it's for torture. Nero reportedly coated some Christians in pine tar and wax before setting them on fire in the arena.

It's also unclear why the company must perform executions for free. One guess is that it's part of the price they pay for getting a monopoly on being the only legal undertakers in town. If they want to get paid as undertakers, they have to volunteer as executioners.

FUNERAL PORTRAIT of man from North Africa, from the AD 200s. Tertullian lived in North Africa about the same time.

CHAPTER 10

"CHRISTIANS HAVE A COMPLETE CROSS"

—TERTULLIAN (ABOUT AD 155–240)

*Christian lawyer and writer who produced
Christianity's first extensive library of writings*

Romans said Christians were crazy for treating the cross like it was something holy. Romans thought Christians were worshiping the cross. This seemed just as insane to Romans as it would seem to us today for anyone to worship the kind of machete a terrorist uses to behead infidels.

Tertullian, a creative thinker and apologist for the Christian faith, came up with a surprising tactic for answering the Romans.

He didn't start by trying to explain that Christians don't worship the cross. Instead, he accused the Romans of worshiping a cross, too.

That probably got their attention.

> You say we are devoted to a cross. Well, you are devoted to a cross, too. The cross is made from wood. You worship wood. The wood you worship comes in the shape of a human. For us, we let the wood be wood. . . .
>
> A beam of wood planted straight up from the ground is just part of a cross, though the largest part. But the cross that people associate with Christians is a complete cross. It comes with a crossbeam and plank as a seat [to prolong the torture]. . . .

HE INVENTED THE WORD *TRINITY*

Quintus Septimius Florens Tertullianus, from what is now the North African nation of Libya, was a Christian lawyer who knew how to juice up his words to defend Christianity and shred its enemies.

He abandoned traditional Christians and hooked up with an offshoot called Montanists—try to imagine intolerant Puritans who spoke in a spiritual language but would tell you bluntly in your own language that you broke the rules and were headed to hell.

Tertullian didn't convert to Christianity until he was about 40 years old. By then, he was a lawyer, educated in Rome. That's where he got curious about Christianity.

For the next two decades he devoted himself to writing. He helped turn Latin, the language of Rome, into the language of Christianity. He used the language well, creating his own fiery style that hooked readers and entertained them with wit, puns, and sarcasm.

He coined phrases and words, *Trinity* among them. Though the Bible refers to God the Father, Son, and Holy Spirit, the Bible writers never used the word *Trinity*. By creating that word, Tertullian did what theo-

---

You don't seem aware of the fact that the images of your gods start with a cross, an instrument of torture. . . . When artisans begin shaping the object to look like a person, they first shape the wood into the figure of a cross. That's because the very structure of the human body is built upon the cross. There's a head at the top. The spine is the upright beam. The shoulders are the crossbeam. When you make an image of a man with his arms stretched out, you have created a picture of a cross.

The artisan starts with a cross and covers it with clay, gradually layering it to create limbs. . . . The artisan slowly transforms the cross into the image of a god later baked hard into ceramic or shaped into marble or cast into bronze or silver or whatever material the artisan decides to use. From the cross to the clay and from the clay to a god. There you have it. With the help of some clay, the cross becomes your god. . . .

This pile of images you have created and your fetish for covering the images in gold is no more than cheap jewelry hanging on a cross. . . . It seems to me you are ashamed to worship a simple cross, as though it might seem a little too naked for you.

To the Nations (*Ad Nationes*), 1.12

logians and other Christian teachers have been doing for 2,000 years: inventing words so they can talk about what they don't understand and can't explain.

Tertullian wasn't into compromise. He advised Christians who were threatened with martyrdom to see it through. He called it God's will.

One of his most famous works, *Against Marcion*, was an attack on a Christian sect led by an excommunicated heavy donor to the church, Marcion (AD 85–160). Marcion taught that the Old Testament God was a nasty and vengeful god. Marcion also compiled his own limited and heavily edited version of New Testament books. His version of a Bible helped spur other church leaders to begin work on compiling their own list of New Testament contenders.

Tertullian was probably in his early 60s when he left the traditional Christian church and joined a group led by the prophet Montanus, from what is now Turkey. Tertullian didn't stay with them. The sect wasn't rigid enough for him. He didn't want Christianity to compromise in any way with the world's culture and beliefs. So he started his own sect, which lasted for about 200 years.

CROSS, FRONT AND CENTER. A painting of Jesus on the cross hangs framed in elegance at the front of St. Dionysius Church in Esslingen, Germany. When Romans accused Christians of worshiping the cross, Tertullian offered a surprise rebuttal: he said the Romans did, too.

CRUCIFIED FOR AN HOUR
—GAIUS VALERIUS CATTULUS (ABOUT 84–54 BC)

Roman poet with an avant-garde style that rattled cages of people who preferred poems about heroes to poetry about everyday life

Cattulus wasn't your normal Roman or Greek poet, writing songs and poems about gods and the heroes they enabled.

He wrote about women. He wrote about life. He even wrote puns.

Here's part of a poem he wrote about a man complaining that his lady has done him wrong. The man compares the torture the woman puts him through to an hour of crucifixion:

> Juventius Honey, I stole a kiss from you while you were playing.
> Mmm, a kiss more delicious than the sweetest nectar.
> You made me pay. I spent a torturous hour
> Crucified, hanging from the top of a huge cross.
> I apologized. You left me hanging.
> My tears did nothing to dampen your fiery anger. . . .
> That sweet kiss of ambrosia
> Now tastes like horseradish.
> Thanks to your miserable punishment for my miserable love
> I'll never steal another kiss from you.
>
> "Carmen 99"

CHAPTER 11

"THEY WERE NAILED TO THE CROSS UPSIDE DOWN"

—EUSEBIUS (ABOUT AD 260–340)

*Bishop, theologian, and
Christianity's first historian*

Jews were to Hitler what Christians were to Roman Emperor Diocletian (AD 244–311). This emperor spent eight years (AD 303–311) trying to wipe out the church. In the process, he created a purge of Christians that became the longest and bloodiest in the history of the Roman Empire.

It was also the last. He failed to destroy the Christian movement. Not only did he fail to kill it but he seemed to give it a boost up. A little more than a decade later, by AD 324, a new emperor named Constantine legalized Christianity. It quickly became the Empire's favorite religion.

ENGRAVING OF EUSEBIUS. No image of the scholar has survived.

CHRISTIANITY CONQUERS THE PAGAN ROMAN EMPIRE

Much of what we know about the first 300 years of the Christian movement—which included blood-red storms of persecution and martyrdom—we know because of Eusebius.

In ten volumes of his encyclopedia called *Church History*, one thing he wants to make sure we don't miss is that the persecuted Christian movement defeated the sprawling, pagan Roman Empire. Beat up, bloodied, and martyred, Christians had followed Jesus all the way to peace at last.

The Roman Empire finally embraced Christianity, making it legal during the reign (AD 306–337) of Emperor Constantine.

Eusebius told the story of how the church got there.

Sadly, we know little about Eusebius beyond that he became the bishop of an outlawed religion. He served in a dangerous location: Israel's Mediterranean coastal city of Caesarea, which Rome designated as its regional capital.

As Eusebius tells it, intense Christian persecution rolled in on them like unpredictable storms—hurricanes we could name after emperors who were particularly interested in eliminating this illegal movement.

In AD 303, when Eusebius was in his early 40s, Diocletian ordered his officials to target Christians in what became known as the Great Persecution. Eusebius's mentor, a scholar named Pamphilus, was arrested, tortured, and in AD 309 martyred. Eusebius was arrested too, but when the storm of persecution died with Diocletian in AD 311, he was released. Two years later he became bishop of Caesarea.

After Christians won the battle with Rome, they started fighting battles among themselves. Sects emerged with oddball teachings. A man named Arius led one of the most threatening movements. He taught that in the beginning, Jesus was not there.

Eusebius, a peacemaker, tried at the Council of Nicea to help traditional church leaders work out their differences with the Arian leaders. Didn't happen. The Arian movement got tagged non-Christian, yet it grew widely popular and came dangerously close to assimilating traditional Christianity into its collective.

Cue Bishop Athanasius. He came along and wrote a letter in AD 367 listing—for the first time on record—every one of the books Christians now have in the New Testament. He said these were the books Christians should trust as inspired by God and inspiring.

One of those books dealt a crushing blow to the Arian movement: "In the beginning the Word already existed. The Word was with God, and the Word was God. . . . So the Word became human and made his home among us" (John 1:1, 14).

Church historian Eusebius describes how Christian martyrs died during Emperor Diocletian's empire-wide persecution of the church. Eusebius writes that he witnessed some of the torture and execution:

> I was there when it happened. I have written it down. I wanted a record of our martyred Savior's power, the power of Jesus Christ. That's because it was His power on display when these martyrs died. . . .
>
> I'm going to tell you about how one person died. And I'll let readers draw their own conclusions about how others may have died. The man was brought before rulers in Nicomedia [a city in what is now northern Turkey]. They ordered him to make a Roman-style sacrifice. He refused. On orders of the rulers, he was stripped, raised high off the ground, and beaten with rods over his entire body. They did this to convince him to do as he was told, even though he didn't want to do it.
>
> Torture wasn't enough to change his mind. Some of his bones had already broken through the skin. People torturing him mixed some vinegar with salt and poured it over the open wounds. But the man endured the agony and refused to break.
>
> His torturers brought out a huge barbecue-like grill, with the fire burning. They put his body on it as though they were going to grill him for a meal. But they didn't put him on it all at once, in a way that would have killed him quickly. They put him on it a little bit at a time. They were ordered not to stop until he agreed to do as he was told.
>
> He knew what he believed, and he believed it all the way to the victorious end of his life, tortured to death. . . .

CHRISTIANS IN THE BULLSEYE. Marble bust of Roman Emperor Diocletian (ruled AD 284–305). He targeted Christians in what became known as the Great Persecution. Eusebius barely escaped—thanks to Diocletian dying.

Thousands of men, women, and children in many nations have been martyred. They died because when they were forced to make a choice between giving up the teachings of our Savior or giving up their life, they chose Jesus.

Some had their skin scraped off. Some were stretched on the rack or severely beaten. So many methods of torture. Too many to count. Some are even difficult to merely hear about.

People were burned alive. Some were drowned in the sea. Some bravely stretched out their neck to people who cut off their heads. Some died of other tortures. Some starved to death.

Some were crucified. Among those, some were crucified in the normal way—the method used for crucifying criminals. But others were crucified in a way that's viciously cruel. They were nailed to the cross upside down and then kept alive until they starved to death.

Church History 6.2–4; 7.2; 8.1–2

STARVING UPSIDE DOWN. Peter is crucified upside down in Rome, according to early church writers. He apparently wasn't the only one killed that way. Church historian Eusebius reported that among the Christians he personally saw martyred, some "were nailed to the cross upside down and then kept alive until they starved to death."

CHAPTER 12

"WE SEE THE SIGN OF THE CROSS NATURALLY OCCURRING IN OUR WORLD"

—MARCUS MINUCIUS FELIX
(DIED ABOUT AD 250)

Roman lawyer who wrote in defense of the Christian faith

Minucius Felix, nearly lost to history, is remembered for one thing: Octavius, a fictional conversation he wrote between a Christian and non-Christian about Christianity.

During that conversation he describes the shape of the cross. Many students of history argue that Jesus died on a stake, since that is a common meaning of the Greek word the Bible writers used—*stauros*. But Minucius Felix paints a word picture of a cross, complete with a crossbar:

> You say that we Christians worship a criminal and the cross on which he died. I'm telling you that you are not even in the right village. . . . We don't worship crosses and we certainly don't want to die on one. . . .

It's true that we see the sign of the cross naturally occurring in our world. We see it on a ship when wind catches the sails on the mast and pushes the ship forward with oars stretched out. We see it when you set up a military yoke [two spears upright and one across the top]. We see it, too, when a man stretches out his arms to worship God. This is the sign of the cross.

Octavius of Minucius Felix, 29

THE CROSS IS EVERYWHERE. Minucius Felix said Christians see "the sign of the cross naturally occurring in our world. We see it on a ship when the wind catches the sails on the mast." The mosaic is from the AD 100s in Tunisia, a North African coastal city south of Italy.

CHAPTER 13

"SAILORS CRUCIFIED THEIR COMMANDING OFFICER"

—Titius Livius, aka Livy
(about 64 BC–AD 12)

One of Rome's greatest historians, and author
of a history of the Roman Empire preserved
in a collection of 142 books

Some 250 years before Jesus was born, the Romans built a navy.

When they fought their first sea battle, it was against an experienced and confident African navy: seasoned sailors from the Carthage Empire headquartered in the North African coastal city of Carthage, in what is now Tunisia. The Carthaginians planned to introduce themselves to the Roman rookies as the boss of the Mediterranean Sea.

Commanding the Carthage navy was a general named Hannibal Gisco, not *the* Hannibal who a

ENGRAVING OF LIVY from the 1500s by Nicolas Beatrizet.

generation later nearly defeated the Roman Empire by marching an army with elephants over the Alps and into northern Italy. This earlier Hannibal was a wartime loser. His garrison got overrun by Romans in the first major battle of the First Punic War, the 262 BC Battle of Agigentum, in Sicily.

Two years later, he commanded a fleet that engaged the rookie Roman navy fighting its first major sea battle. Hannibal lined up his ships in the conventional way. Romans didn't. They used land warfare tactics. They equipped their ships with a portable ladder-like bridge for boarding other ships. They won. Hannibal retreated.

Two years after that, Hannibal's superior officers ordered him to defend the island of Sardinia against Roman invasion. He couldn't stop the Roman fleet. After he failed, his sailors apparently didn't want to go sailing into battle with him again.

Here's a passing note about what happened next. It comes from Livy. Sadly, we don't know the whole story because all we get is a summary of what Livy wrote about the battle. He wrote about the history of Rome in a massive collection called *History*. The full set: 142 books. But books 11–20 and 46–142 have been lost. The story of the losing general Hannibal shows up in lost book 17. We know this because another book from the AD 300s, *Periochae*, summarizes all 142 books, adding this note:

> Carthaginian sailors crucified their commanding officer, Hannibal, after he led them into another defeat.
>
> *Periochae*, 17.257

Some historians suggest that the Romans may have gotten their idea for crucifixion from the Carthaginians.

CRUCIFYING THE WRONG-WAY GUIDE

A second Hannibal came along a generation later. Some historians say he was the greatest military strategist of all time. That's partly because he managed not only to sneak his African army into Italy by the scenic route, over the Spanish Pyrenees mountains and the snowcapped Swiss

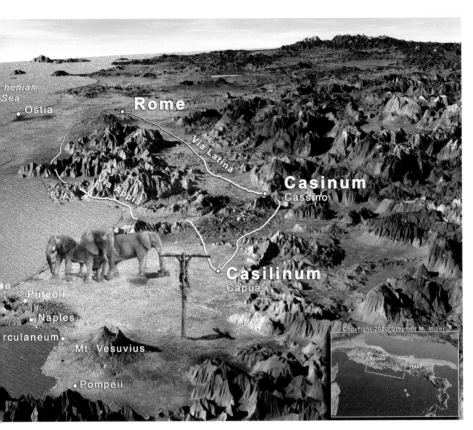

HANNIBAL, LOST WITH ELEPHANTS. Hannibal's guide, who was either a spy or someone who had trouble understanding Hannibal's African twang, took Hannibal's army to the wrong town that starts with a "C." Instead of camping at Casinum, where they would have controlled a major route into Rome, they wintered in Casilinum, a sprawling coastal bay where they got trapped between Romans in the hills and Romans in the deep blue sea. Hannibal crucified the guide and lost the war. One elephant of an estimated 80 survived the battles.

Alps, but he did it accompanied by an elephant cavalry, estimated by some at 80—each one armored for battle.

Hannibal also commanded an infantry of at least 20,000 soldiers and a horse cavalry of about 6,000. Along the way he picked up Roman rebel forces as allies. He grew an army of about 100,000 men who stampeded with him throughout much of Italy, from north to south.

During one of his campaigns in southern Italy, he ordered his guide to lead them back north to the territory of Casinum, now Cassino, about 80 miles (125 km) south of Rome.

The guide never quite got them there.

> Some people who knew the area well told Hannibal to go there [Casinum]. They said if he controlled the pass through the mountains he could block Romans from advancing to help their allies.
> Carthaginians, however, had trouble pronouncing Latin names.
> The guide misunderstood Hannibal's order. Instead of leading the army to Casinum, the guide took them to Casilinum [near what is now Capua, 30 miles (50 km) in the opposite direction—putting them more than 100 miles (160 km) south of Rome]. . . .
> Hannibal looked around at the wide-open fields with rivers and with some mountains nearby, and he wanted to know where on earth his guide had taken him. He called the man in and ordered him to explain himself. The guide reassured Hannibal that he would spend the night in Casilinum. That's the moment Hannibal realized that the guide had made a huge mistake. Casinum was way off in the opposite direction from where Hannibal wanted to go.
> Hannibal ordered the guide beaten. And then to put a little fear of the general into everyone, Hannibal ordered the guide crucified.
>
> *History of Rome*, 22.13

CHAPTER 14

"HIS ARMS STRETCHED OUT ON A CROSS"

—LACTANTIUS (AD 240–320)

Christian writer and advisor to Roman Emperor Constantine, who legalized Christianity

Pacifist at heart, Christian philosopher Lucius Caecilius Firmianus Lactantius wrote in his most famous theology book, *Divine Institutes*, that Christians shouldn't serve in the army or charge anyone with a capital offense. He said God prohibits killing. "No exception."

Lactantius took it further. He said that when people come to hurt us, we shouldn't resist. He also said we shouldn't allow death threats to convince us to do something we know is unjust or against God's law.

LACTANTIUS. Considered one of the church fathers who helped establish the Christian church, Lactantius advised Roman Emperor Constantine, who legalized the faith and adopted it as the empire's favored religion.

If someone tries to bully us into deserting God and betraying our Christian faith, it's better to die than to give in to that. We need to defend our spiritual freedom in the face of foolish and violent people who don't have the sense it takes to mind their own business. In the face of all threats and terror we muscle up our spirit and stand strong in our faith. . . .

Seneca says this in his books of moral behavior:

> I'll tell you what an honorable man is like. I'm not talking about someone highly regarded because of his high office or because he has an entourage of people following him and serving him. But I am talking about someone who's every bit as honorable.
>
> This is a man who stays calm even when he sees he's about to die. He stands face to face with death, but he doesn't even look surprised.
>
> He might have to suffer torture all over his body. He might have to open his mouth for fire [possibly a torch or molten metal]. He might even have to stretch out his arms on a cross. But he doesn't question why he suffers. Instead, he does his best to suffer well.
>
> *Divine Institutes,* 6.17, 6.20

"CHRISTIANS CAN'T KILL." A soldier stands guard at the crucifixion of Jesus. Theology scholar Lactantius said Christians should be willing to die rather than serve in the military or charge anyone with a capital offense. A Christian who is that devoted to Jesus, Lactantius admitted, "might have to suffer torture all over his body. . . . He might even have to stretch out his arms on a cross."

CHAPTER 15

"THE SOLDIER ... SAW THAT ONE OF THE CROSSES HAD LOST ITS CORPSE"

—PHAEDRUS (ABOUT 15 BC–AD 50)

Roman author of fables and possibly a former
slave freed by Emperor Augustus

"The Widow of Ephesus," also known as "The Widow and the Soldier," was written as a fun story for sailors. At the expense of the ladies. And set within sight of an active crucifixion.

So it's not gender-sensitive and it's not respectful of the dead, which may be why Phaedrus treated it as entertainment for a crew of sailors.

The point of the story, the narrator says, is to prove that women are fickle. In fact, he essentially says when they get a chance, they protect their intimacy like sailors on leave.

A narrator tells the story:

> A gorgeous lady lived in Ephesus [a city on what is now the west coast of Turkey]. She was so doggone gorgeous that even women from neighboring villages came to look at her. Regarding matters of sex, she was a saint, absolutely devoted to her husband. Everyone knew it.
>
> When her husband died, she wasn't content to simply attend

the funeral and mourn in the usual way, messing up her hair and beating on her naked breasts in front of a crowd.

She went to the tomb and absolutely refused to leave, day or night. She would not be consoled by friends and relatives and city officials. She would not eat or drink. . . .

In the meantime, the governor sentenced some robbers to be hung from crosses near where the woman was wailing over the corpse. That night, a soldier stood guard by the crosses to make sure no one pulled a corpse off and buried it. He saw a light by the tomb and he heard the woman groaning. Curiosity, a common weakness of humans, got the better of him. He wanted to know what was going on over there.

He left his post and went down to the tomb. There he saw a

COME TO THE CRUCIFIXION SHOW

An ad for crucifixion as entertainment has survived 2,000 years.

Fortunately, it was posted on a wall in the unfortunate city of Pompeii a few years before Mount Vesuvius blew an estimated 600 yards (meters) off its top in AD 79, sealing Pompeii in a time capsule of volcanic ash.

The advertisement—oddly enough, posted in a graveyard—promoted the kind of grisly spectacle we might expect to see acted out in a movie about Roman gladiators and sociopathic officials numb to the misery of others.

Placement of the ad between some tombs was probably a good idea from a marketing standpoint. The tombs were located just outside one of the main entrances into Pompeii: the Nucerian Gate. Lots of traffic there.

Some words and parts of words are missing from the ad, which promotes the spectacle at Cumae (now Cuma), a city about 30 miles (50 km) northwest of Pompeii (see map page 111). But scholars say it looks as though the ad may have communicated the following basic information:

Event location: Cumae arena

Show dates: October 1, 5–7

Featured event: Twenty pairs of gladiators will fight. Backup substitutes will be available if needed [perhaps to take the place of gladiators who were supposed to fight, but couldn't].

Also featuring: Crucifixions and a fight with wild animals

Bonus: Covered awning above the arena

Promotion by: Cuniculus, who says hello to Lucceio

woman so beautiful that it terrified him. He thought she was a ghost or a being from the other side. But then he saw the dead man lying in the tomb and he could see the woman's tears and the scratches she had made on her face with her fingernails. He quickly figured out what was going on. The woman simply didn't want to live without her husband.

The soldier brought her some of his food and pleaded with her to move past the grieving and to stop sobbing and tearing at herself. He said, "We all end up here.". . . The woman, weak from many days of fasting, finally gave in and ate food with a passion. . . .

Now you all know what tempts people once they get their stomach nice and full. Tactics the soldier had used to convince

LAST MAN STANDING. With the battle of the gladiators over, a winner looks to the emperor for thumbs up or thumbs down.

the woman to keep on living are the same tactics he used to show her how to live it up. . . .

They spent quality time together that night and privately married, pledging vows to each other. They spent a second night together. They spent a third night together. They shut the doors of the burial vault so people would think she was one of the most devoted wives of all, choosing to die with her husband.

As for the soldier, he was having a great time. The woman was stunning, even in a tomb. And there was something wickedly enjoyable about the secrecy of this love affair. Every day he bought little presents for the woman and gave them to her at nighttime.

Out where the crucified bodies hung, parents of one of the crucified criminals noticed that the guards were slacking off. The parents dragged down the corpse and gave it a proper burial.

That's how the soldier got taken, while he was absent without leave. The next day when he saw that one of the crosses had lost its corpse, he was terrified. He told the woman that he wasn't going to wait around for any court-martial and execution. He said he would punish himself with his own sword.

He told her to find a place for him to die and that this would be the burial place for both of them.

The woman said, "Not on your life. I'll be darned if I'm going to look on the dead bodies of the two men I love most. I'd rather crucify the dead than kill the living."

She told the soldier to take the body of her husband out of tomb and attach it to the empty cross.

This ingenious woman had hit on a marvelously creative idea. The soldier did as he was told. The next day, everyone in town wondered how in the world the dead man managed to get himself out of the tomb and up on the cross.

The sailors had a good laugh about the story. . . . Lycas, however, did not laugh at all. He said, "If the governor had any sense of justice, he would have ordered someone to take the man's body off the cross and carry it back to the tomb. Then he would have crucified that woman."

"Widow of Ephesus,"
Satyricon of Petronius Arbiter, 111–113

CHAPTER 16

"LAUREOLUS, HANGING ON A CROSS, SPILLED HIS GUTS TO A SCOTTISH BEAR"

—MARTIAL (ABOUT AD 38–102)

Roman poet who wrote over 1,500 short satires, poking fun at the people and the times

It wasn't always entertaining enough to watch gladiators slash and slam each other to death. Crucifixion was even less entertaining. After the nailing, there wasn't much left to watch but someone hanging around.

Spectacle producers added theatrical effects.

They sometimes created a storyline with a plot and characters, good and bad. They added music and props, and they built extravagant sets. They put on horror shows, by our standards. Lion hunts. Famous battles reenacted, with people dying for real. Executions reenacted of famous criminals.

Marcus Valerius Martialis— *Martial* for short

One villain whose story the Romans reenacted was a man named Laureolus. As the story goes, whether true or not, he was a notorious robber who ended up crucified. While he hung there, wild animals attacked him, tearing him to fleshy shreds.

Another man whose name is lost to history had the misfortune of starring in the remake of that story. It was one of the featured acts that entertained Romans at the dedication of the famous Colosseum at Rome in about AD 80.

Martial wrote about it in a collection of notes and poems called "On the Spectacles":

> Just as the god Prometheus, tied to a Sythean rock,
> fed a bird every day with pieces from his immortal body,
> Laureolus, hanging on a cross,
> spilled his guts to a Scottish bear.
> With mangled arms and legs quivering, slobbered in blood,
> the man's body was gone, shapeless as gore.
> Punishment he suffered would fit the crime
> of a man who murdered his parents
> or a slave who slashed his master's throat
> or a thief who stole the temple gold
> or an arsonist who put the torch to our dear Rome.
> Whatever his crime, and who cares what it was,
> must have been the worst of all, given what he got.
> For the crowds, it was a play. For him, an execution.
>
> *On the Spectacles*, 9.7

CHAPTER 17

"SIX THOUSAND SURRENDERED. CRASSUS CRUCIFIED THEM ALL"

—APPIAN OF ALEXANDRIA
(ABOUT AD 95–165)

Greek historian, citizen of Rome, and author of a 24-volume series called Roman History

Romans wanted everyone to remember Spartacus, the gladiator who led a slave rebellion against Rome. Here's the scene they had in mind.

Imagine a short stretch of road about the length of a football field. Now picture three people crucified on crosses along the sidelines. One beside an end zone. Another on the fifty-yard line. And a third beside the other end zone. Now extend this road for 120 miles (180 km) with 6,000 crucified people.

A Roman general sent a message to the rest of the world by ordering these crosses posted alongside one of the Roman Empire's main highways into Rome, the Appian Way. The crucifixions started in

APPIAN gets a bit lost among other Roman historians. But he wrote a gripping history about Spartacus, and the slave revolt that nearly defeated Rome.

the city of Capua near Naples and they ended at Rome (see map page 111).

That's the dramatic, final scene in Spartacus's story. He is presumed dead because his body was never found. The last of his army, the surviving 6,000, ended their days dying slowly on crosses along the Appian Way.

Spartacus was born a Thracian [a territory along the borders of Bulgaria, Turkey, and Greece]. He had served as a soldier in the Roman army, but he deserted, was captured, and was sold as a gladiator.

It was in the gladiatorial training facility at Capua that he convinced about seventy of his fellow gladiators to fight for their freedom instead of fighting for the amusement of an audience.

They surprised and overpowered the guards, and escaped. They took clubs and knives from people as they headed to Mount Vesuvius, where they made their camp.

DEAD ARMY OF SPARTACUS. After crushing the rebel army of slaves led by Spartacus, Roman general Licinius Crassus lined a main road to Rome—120 miles (180 km) of the Appian Way—with 6,000 crucified captives.

Word spread about their escape. Runaway slaves joined them, as well as free citizens who left their work in the fields. . . .

Romans didn't realize they were in a war yet. They treated Spartacus and the others like a gang of robbers. They sent some soldiers in a policing action. The Romans attacked Spartacus but lost the battle. . . . Word of his victory spread and even more people rushed to join him. His army swelled to 70,000.

Rome responded by sending two legions [10,000 soldiers] against him. . . . He beat them and scattered them in all directions.

His army grew to 120,000. That's when he marched on Rome. He burned all of his nonessential supplies, executed all of his prisoners, and butchered the pack animals that would have slowed him down. . . . Spartacus later changed his mind about going to Rome. He decided his army was not yet ready for a battle like that. . . .

Three years into the war, there was only one Roman soldier volunteering to march against Spartacus. The man was Licinius Crassus, a rich noble who took six legions [30,000 soldiers]. . . .

As the two opposing armies stood face-to-face, Spartacus took a captured Roman soldier into no-man's land between the armies. There he crucified the soldier. He did this to show his own men what was going to happen to them if they did not win this war. . . .

The last battle was long and bloody. Anyone should expect as much from so many thousands of desperate men fighting for their lives and for the lives of their families.

Spartacus took a spear to the thigh and dropped down on a knee. He remained there in a defensive position holding his shield in front of him until he and his crowd of fighters were surrounded, overrun, and slaughtered.

Romans lost about 1,000 men in the lopsided victory. The body of Spartacus was never recovered.

Thousands of his men escaped to the mountains. Crassus hunted them down and continued to fight them until the final 6,000 surrendered. Crassus crucified them all along the road from Capua to Rome.

Roman History, 1.116–121

GAIUS SUETONIUS TRANQUILLUS

CHAPTER 18

"HE ORDERED THE MAN CRUCIFIED ON A CROSS ... PAINTED WHITE"

—SUETONIUS (ABOUT AD 69–126)

Roman historian best known for writing the history of twelve Roman rulers: Julius Caesar to Domitian

After Emperor Nero committed suicide, a retired military officer named Galba took over. He had retired during Nero's reign, but was later assigned to govern what is now northern Spain.

During his stint in Spain, he sometimes punished people a little more than necessary.

Galba governed the province for eight years. But he wasn't consistent in the way he governed or in the way he punished offenders.

He put a lot into the job at first. He sometimes went overboard when it came time to punish someone. He cut off the hands of a banker who was cheating people and he nailed the man's hands to the countertop.

Then there was the guardian who poisoned to death the young man he was supposed to be protecting. The guardian did that because he was in line to inherit the young man's estate. Galba ordered him crucified.

The man objected. He invoked his privilege as a Roman citizen, since it was illegal to crucify a citizen.

Galba agreed to reduce the sentence out of respect for the man's Roman citizenship. He ordered the man crucified on a cross that executioners painted white and elevated higher than the others.

Galba gradually backed off in his governing style because he didn't want to give Nero any reason to think of him as the competition.

The Life of Galba, 9.1

After Nero died, Rome's Praetorian Guard, the emperor's elite corps of bodyguards, backed Galba as Nero's successor. They quickly tired of the 71-year-old man and withdrew their support after seven months. He died assassinated by his successor, Ortho, a nobleman who didn't seem particularly noble.

CRUCIFIED FOR BRINGING THE WRONG GIFT

Some people can't say a simple thank you for a gift pig.

One such man was a Roman governor of Sicily named Lucius Domitius Ahenobarbus. He ruled the island nation in the late 90s BC, shortly after the Second Servile War (104–100 BC), a failed revolt among slaves on the island.

Domitius was a stickler for the rules. When he governed Sicily as praetor, a shepherd brought him the gift of a huge boar.

Domitius wanted to meet that shepherd, so he ordered someone to go and get him. When the shepherd got there, Domitius asked him how he killed the boar. When Domitius found out that the shepherd used a hunting spear, he crucified the man.

It was illegal for the people to bear arms. Domitius had banned weapons because he wanted to keep them away from gangs and rebels who caused trouble all over the island.

Valerius Maximus, Of Words and Deeds, 6.3.5

PART 2

WHAT ROMANS SAID ABOUT JESUS'S CRUCIFIXION

NO EYEWITNESSES ON RECORD. Few scholars of history doubt that Romans crucified the man whose teachings launched the Christian movement. But we have nothing in writing—in or out of the Bible—from someone who claims to have witnessed Jesus's crucifixion. The disciple John, portrayed here with Mary the mother of Jesus, wrote the gospel of John, according to early church leaders. But the gospel writer—whoever he was—decided to remain anonymous, like the other three gospel writers.

There's no such thing as an eyewitness report of Jesus's crucifixion.

Not in Roman history.

Not in the Bible, not as far as we can be certain. Many Christian Bible scholars would agree with that, probably most.

Roman historians from the first Christian century wrote briefly about Jesus and the crucifixion. But they seemed to have gotten their information from other people, much like historians do today.

Ditto for Bible writers; at least that's a common guess among Christian New Testament scholars. The four gospels of Matthew, Mark, Luke, and John—which report stories and teachings about Jesus—were written by people who chose not to identify themselves. It's possible some of them saw the crucifixion of Jesus. Many say John, one of Jesus's closest disciples and a best friend, likely wrote the gospel of John and described the Crucifixion as he personally witnessed it. Early church writers credited John with the book. But none of the Bible writers went on record to identify themselves and to say they saw Jesus crucified.

The anonymous writer of the gospel of Luke all but admits he never met Jesus. Early church tradition identifies the writer as Paul's traveling associate, a physician named Luke. That's where the book got its name. Luke didn't show up on Christian radar until a couple of decades after the Crucifixion, when he joined Paul's ministry: "Only Luke is with me" (2 Timothy 4:11 NLT, NIV, NASB).

Whoever wrote the gospel of Luke says he got his information from others, through careful research:

> Many people have set out to write accounts about the events that have been fulfilled among us. They used the eyewitness reports circulating among us from the early disciples. Having carefully investigated everything from the beginning, I also have decided to write an accurate account for you. (Luke 1:1–3)

Then Luke starts at the beginning of Jesus's life by telling the now-famous Christmas story of Baby Jesus, born in Bethlehem.

Some critics of Christianity say there's not enough evidence to suggest that Jesus was anything more than a myth—a spark of imagination that lit a fire under some Jews, convincing them that the Messiah had come and died and rose from the dead.

Those critics must deal with what first-century Roman writers said about Jesus. Granted, those Romans didn't say much. But what they did say puts Jesus on the map—and on the cross.

"A WISE MAN CALLED JESUS APPEARED"

—Josephus, Jewish historian

Flavius Josephus is the headliner. (See his story on page 59). He gets top billing for the most famous quote about Jesus that shows up in a book other than the Bible.

The problem is whether to file the quote under history or Christian propaganda—fact or fiction. Scholars and other students of the Bible make engaging arguments from both sides of that shouting match.

Scholars nicknamed the famous quote after Flavius Josephus: *Testimonium Flavianum*. That's Latin for the *Testimony of Flavius*.

There's also the question of which version to trust: the old manuscripts written in Greek or the Syrian manuscripts written in Arabic.

The Greek version makes Josephus sound like a Christian sympathizer—if not a Christian.

The theory explaining this quote goes like this. Somewhere along history's timeline, one or more well-meaning Christians edited the original to make Josephus sound theologically pleasant.

Greek version, with suspicious words in italics:

About this time a wise man called Jesus appeared, *if it's right to call him just a man*. He did astonishing things. He taught the kind of men who were delighted to hear the truth. He attracted

Jews as well as non-Jews. He convinced many people to follow him. *He was the Messiah [Christ, in Greek].* Pilate, acting on the request of our top [Jewish] leaders, sentenced him to crucifixion on the cross. Yet the people who loved this man didn't give up on him. *He came back to life on the third day and appeared to them, just as the godly prophets had predicted. This was just one of the 10,000 wonderful insights they taught about him.* The Christian movement, named after him, hasn't died out.

Antiquities of the Jews, 18.3.3

The oldest surviving copies of this book dates to the AD 1000s. Earliest known mention, AD 300s. This paraphrased excerpt is from Greek

BONE BOX FOR BROTHER OF JESUS. Bones of "James, son of Joseph, brother of Jesus" may have rested in this casket-like limestone box.

Scholars say the burial box, an ossuary that an antiquities dealer made public in 2002, dates sometime between the first century BC and AD 70, the year Romans levelled Jerusalem.

In Bible times, bodies decomposed inside a tomb. Then someone put the bones in a bone box like this, making room in the tomb for other family members who died.

Scholars say they disagree about whether the inscription is authentic. The Israel Antiquities Authority quickly declared it a fake in 2003. But two scholars specializing in inscriptions from this time said it's the real thing, and written in the Aramaic language that Jesus and many other Jews spoke. If it is authentic, it's the first known reference to Jesus.

copies of Josephus's book, in a section that most historians agree editors later Christianized and made Jewish Josephus sound like a good Christian gentleman.

The Syrian version leaves Josephus sounding neutral, like an objective historian. Many scholars say this version provides at least the basic facts Josephus reported, if not the authentic quote itself.

> Syrian version, which quotes Josephus:
>
> About this time a wise man called Jesus appeared. He was a good person, with a reputation for spiritual integrity. A lot of Jews became his disciples. So did people from other countries. Pilate sentenced him to death by crucifixion. The disciples of Jesus didn't give up on him. They kept believing what he taught them. They said he appeared to them after his crucifixion—and that he was alive. Because of this, Jesus may have been the Messiah that the prophets had predicted would come and do miracles.
>
> *Book of History (Kitab al-'Unwan)*, part 2

This is a paraphrase of Agapius (who died about AD 942), a Christian historian who quoted Josephus's *Antiquities of the Jews*. This Syrian version gives the impression that Josephus was a writer preserving the story, but not necessarily buying into it.

CRITICS ENTER HERE

Scholars turn to Josephus when they want to know what was going on in the Roman Empire during the first century. He wrote thirty or more books published by the early AD 90s.

Scholars don't expect Josephus to get everything perfectly right. They allow for human error, exaggerations, and even some grandstanding. But generally, they treat Josephus's reporting as factual, and they cite those facts in the classes they teach and in the academic papers and journal articles they write.

There's one staggering exception: Josephus's short reference to Jesus—the paragraph known as *Testimonium Flavianum*, Latin for the

JOSEPHUS IDs JOHN THE BAPTIST AND JESUS'S BROTHER

Jesus isn't the only member of his family to show up in Josephus's history of the Jews.

One of his brothers is there: James the leader of the Jerusalem church. Josephus reports his execution.

John the Baptist is there, too, a distant relative of Jesus. Their mothers, Mary and Elizabeth, were related, though the Bible doesn't say how (Luke 1:36). Josephus writes about John's death, too.

FAMILY REUNION. Mary and her relative Elizabeth meet after the birth of their boys. Elizabeth gave birth to John the Baptist perhaps six months or more before Mary gave birth to Jesus. Elizabeth was six months pregnant when the angel Gabriel told Mary she would have a son.

Though some scholars say they doubt Josephus wrote the *Testimony*, a short paragraph about Jesus's crucifixion, most seem to agree that the references to James and John are both Genuine Josephus.

THE STONING OF JAMES

Not only do most scholars embrace what Josephus said about the execution of James but they generally prefer his report over a slightly different version written a few decades later by a Christian historian named Hegesippus.

Josephus said that in the early AD 60s, about thirty years after the top Jewish council in Jerusalem orchestrated the crucifixion of Jesus, that same group of Jewish leaders ordered the stoning of "James, the brother of Jesus—the one who was called the Messiah" (*Antiquities of the Jews*, 20.9).

Hegesippus added some grisly details. He said Jewish leaders known as scribes and Pharisees— bitter enemies of Jesus, according to gospel writers—took James to a high point at the Jerusalem temple, possibly at the top of one of the walls.

> They pushed down this good man and then said, "Let's go stone James the Just." And that's what they did. They started to stone him because he didn't die in the fall. James

kneeled in front of them and prayed, "I beg you, Lord God our Father, forgive these people. They don't know what they're doing."

While they continued stoning him to death, one of the priests tried to stop them. . . . He screamed, "Stop! What are you doing? This good man is praying for us." But one man in the group who dyed clothes for a living picked up one of his tools. It was a wooden pole used to wring out the wet cloth he dyed. He swung it like a club, hard and fast at the head of the good man. That's how James was martyred. They buried him where he fell. People erected a pillar there in his memory. It is still standing, near the temple."

Acts of the Church, 5

EXECUTION OF JOHN THE BAPTIST

Josephus, agreeing with Bible writers, says Herod Antipas (who reigned 4 BC–AD 39), son of Herod the Great, ordered John executed.

That's Genuine Josephus, most scholars seem to agree—not the add-on work of some Christian editor centuries later. Scholars say this link between the Bible and history reported outside the Bible is one of the most reliable.

John might not have made the cut in Josephus's history book had it not been for Herod Antipas marrying his sister-in-law. Herod stole his own brother's wife. Herod's first wife didn't like that. She ran back to her father, an Arab king from what is now Jordan. Daddy King went to war with his former son-in-law and decimated Herod's army.

Some Jews blamed Herod's execution of John the Baptist for the defeat, Josephus said.

God destroyed Herod's army to punish him for what he did to John, who was called the Baptist. Herod killed him. John was a good man. He taught the Jews to live as good human beings, both in the way they treated one another and in the reverence they showed toward God.

He told the people to get baptized. He said that washing would purify their bodies and make them acceptable to God. He presumed they had already purified their souls and were living lives devoted to God.

Crowds of people gathered around him, and what he taught them moved them deeply.

This worried Herod. He was afraid John might use his influence over the people to provoke a rebellion. It certainly looked to Herod as though the people would do anything John asked. Herod decided that his best course of action would be to execute John, to keep him from causing any trouble.

Antiquities of the Jews, 18.5.2

Testimony of Flavius Josephus. Many say they don't believe Josephus wrote it. They say Christians inserted it later.

And the debate begins. This short, contested sliver of Josephus's massive collection of writings is probably the most talked about.

Reading through the back-and-forth arguments about the *Testimony* is like biting into a hunk of gristle at dinner on a first date. The more you chew it, the bigger it gets. And you come to realize there's no easy way out of this.

WHY SOME PEOPLE REJECT JOSEPHUS'S JESUS

Some students of history say there's no proof Jesus ever existed, and that there's no mention of him outside the Bible.

That includes the paragraph about him in Josephus's *Antiquities of the Jews* (18.3.3), the *Testimony of Flavius Josephus.*

The oldest complete Greek edition of Josephus's book goes back only about halfway to the time he lived—to about 1,000 years ago. The manuscript, with a name reminiscent of a distant comet nobody cares about—Ambrosianus 370 (F 128)—rests in a library in Milan, Italy: the Biblioteca Ambrosiana.

"He was the Messiah." Some historians would agree that this line is perhaps the best reason to conclude that what we're reading isn't what Josephus was writing.

Even most Christian scholars seem to agree on that.

In Josephus's day, loyal Romans hunted down wannabe Jewish messiahs and crucified them for insurrection, as traitors trying to overthrow Caesar and declare themselves king. Josephus was a loyal Roman—loyal to his adopted dad, Emperor Vespasian (who ruled AD 69–79), and loyal to his adopted brother, who became Emperor Titus (and reigned AD 79–81).

Messiahs weren't loyal to Rome. They were loyal to Israel.

Jews thought of messiahs as warrior kings, like David. Many Jews in the first century taught that God would send a messiah to free the Jews from Roman occupation and to restore the sovereign nation of Israel to its former glory—to the Golden Age of King David and his son King Solomon.

Never happened.

The days of the kings were long gone. Jews would have to wait nearly 2,000 years to regain a foothold in their homeland and then to finally, in 1948, declare themselves a sovereign nation again. Not because of a messiah. But because of a journalist: Theodor Herzl (1860–1904), founder of the Zionist movement who lobbied for a Jewish homeland and who encouraged Jews to migrate there to buy land from Palestinians.

When Jesus arrived, about a century into Rome's occupation of the Jewish homeland, most Jews were fed up with Romans. They wanted their freedom and they expected God to deliver on his promise to send a savior king from David's family.

> A child has been born for us.
> We have been given a son
>   who will be our ruler.
> His name will be
> Wonderful Advisor
>   and Mighty God,
>   Eternal Father
>   and Prince of Peace.
> His power will never end;
>   peace will last forever.
> He will rule David's kingdom
>   and make it grow strong.
> He will always rule
>   with honesty and justice.
> The LORD All-Powerful
> will make certain
>   that all of this is done. (Isaiah 9:6–7 CEV)

Romans did not approve of this message.

Josephus, nearly all historians agree, would never have said that he believed Jesus was the messiah who God promised to send.

Josephus avoided the volatile "M" word, *Messiah*. In Greek it's the "C" word, *Christ*. In Josephus's *Antiquities of the Jews*, the word shows up in references only to Jesus. First, in this disputed paragraph about

Jesus. And second, in a later paragraph about the execution of James, the brother of Jesus, "who was called the Messiah."

Early Christians never mentioned Josephus's* Testimony *about Jesus. This is another reason some scholars say a Christian editor, several centuries after Josephus, inserted the paragraph about Jesus into Josephus's book.

Many church leaders from the first couple of centuries wrote about Josephus and quoted his books. But they never mentioned his reference to Jesus.

If a Christian writer is going to pick one thing to highlight from Josephus, some would think the writer would pick Josephus's report about the crucifixion and resurrection of Jesus.

Here are a few church heavyweights—most of them notable leaders of their day—who wrote about Josephus but never mentioned his *Testimony*, as far as we know.

- Clement of Alexandria, Egypt (about AD 150–215), a theology scholar

- Irenaeus (died about AD 202), Church Father, bishop in France, and theologian

- Marcus Minucius Felix (died about AD 250), writer who defended Christianity

- Origen (about AD 184–253), Church Father, Greek scholar, and Christian theologian

Josephus's* Testimony *about Jesus wasn't mentioned for 300 years. The first human on record to write about the disputed paragraph is Eusebius, a Christian historian and bishop, writing about AD 324.

Eusebius wasn't just the first to mention Josephus's *Testimony*, some scholars add. They say he probably created it from thin air, like a preacher with a fictional sermon illustration passed off as fact.

Others would argue that accusing Eusebius of doing the deed since he was the first to discover the passage is a bit like accusing a man of murder because he was the first to discover the body. Still, it does look suspicious.

The next church leader on record to mention the paragraph came a generation later: Jerome (about AD 347–420), a priest best known for translating most of the Bible into Latin, the language of the Roman Empire. That Bible is called the *Vulgate,* a word that means "common," implying that this Bible was written in the common language of the day. Jerome's version of the *Testimony* reads differently than the version Eusebius quoted. Jerome had Josephus saying that Jesus "was believed to be the Messiah," not that he "was the Messiah."

As for why no Christian writer mentioned the Jesus paragraph before, perhaps they did. It's a weak argument, some say, to assume that since we haven't found anything yet, it doesn't exist. A lot of what the Romans and the early church leaders wrote disappeared. We know that because some of them refer to material that hasn't shown up yet.

On the other hand, maybe church leaders didn't mention the paragraph because they didn't think it was all that important. Josephus didn't say anything new. He was simply a nonbeliever who confirmed the existence of Jesus. Christians already knew Jesus existed, just as we know that George Washington was born almost 300 years ago. We don't need anyone to tell us that.

Besides, Christians had the more complete story of Jesus's crucifixion and resurrection in the writings they later compiled into the New Testament—books they said God inspired. During those centuries, church leaders had to fight their way through stacks of stories about Jesus and his disciples, as they tried to determine which would be most helpful to preserve and to recommend to the growing church. The *Testimony,* a skimpy paragraph from a traitorous Jew, didn't make the cut.

Josephus's Testimony *about Jesus doesn't fit the flow of the story Josephus was telling.* Some historians say the *Testimony* doesn't fit the context of the chapter. Josephus tells a series of one-paragraph stories about Jews getting upset with something the Romans did, rioting about it, and then suffering the consequences.

Then there's a short, comparatively upbeat paragraph about Jesus, crucified and then reportedly rising from the dead.

The outline of Josephus's chapter looks like this.

Story 1: Jews protest Roman idols. Governor Pilate brings images of Caesar to Jerusalem. The images are on military standards—flag-like poles the armies carried. Jews rally in protest because their law forbids engraved images of people (Exodus 20:4). Pilate finally agrees to remove the objects from Jerusalem.

Story 2: Pilate orders Jewish protestors murdered during their protest. Pilate uses money collected at the Jewish temple to build a water channel from a stream to Jerusalem. Ten thousand Jews who apparently aren't that thirsty join the protest. Pilate orders his soldiers to break up the protest by killing many of the unarmed Jews.

Story 3: Pilate crucifies Jesus. Pilate orders Jesus crucified. But the disciples of Jesus report that he rose from the dead. This is the *Testimony.*

Story 4: Woman gets conned into sleeping with a man she thinks is a god. A man in Rome falls in lust with a married woman. He asks her to spend some quality time with him. She refuses. So he hires someone to concoct a way for him to spend the night with her. A woman bribes Isis priests to tell the target lady that Anubis, god of the dead, wants to sleep with her. She and her husband agree. Who can say no to the god of the dead? They later find out they've been had. Emperor Tiberius orders the priests and their briber crucified, the Isis temple destroyed, and the lustful man banished (not killed, since his crime was love). See more about the story on page 69.

Story 5: Emperor bans all Jews from Rome after woman is conned out of temple donations. Four Jewish con artists in Rome present themselves as teachers of the Jewish laws. They talk a rich Roman woman into donating gold and expensive purple fabric to the Jewish temple in Jerusalem. Her donations never make it out of Rome. The Jews keep it for themselves. Emperor Tiberius finds out and he banishes all Jews from Rome—4,000 men. He sends them to the island of Sardinia, where many are forced to become soldiers.

Some historians uncomfortable with Jesus in that lineup of short stories speculate that the paragraph about him may have been, originally, a report about rioting caused by early Christian leaders such as Paul and James, the brother of Jesus.

A defense of the story of Jesus is that it's no less intrusive than the odd story that follows it. If any story seems inappropriate in this chapter, that's the one, some would argue—the story of the lady sleeping with a man who must have had a wonderful evening pretending he was a god. It's the only story in the chapter that doesn't talk about the Jews. At least the story of Jesus follows the pattern of the first two, which spotlights the famous mistakes of Pilate. Crucifying Jesus is just another one of them.

"If it's right to call him just a man." This is another odd statement that shows up in the Greek version of the *Testimony* about Jesus. Just about everyone agrees this is something Josephus would not have written.

The phrase seems to suggest that Jesus must have been a celestial being—if not the divine Son of God, as Christians taught.

A devout, tradition-minded Jew like Josephus would never have said something like that out loud, even if he believed it—which he probably didn't.

There's only one God. That's the most basic Jewish teaching. It's the fundamental belief on which the entire Jewish religion is built:

"The LORD our God is the only true God" (Deuteronomy 6:4 CEV). One God. Not two or three.

The description of Jesus reads like it came from the gospel of Luke. Critics have produced charts that pull Greek phrases out of Josephus's *Testimony* and compare them side-by-side with similar words from the gospel of Luke.

For example, as some scholars translate Josephus, Jesus was someone who performed "amazing deeds." In Greek, that's *"paradoxon ergon."* Luke describes Jesus as "mighty in deed" (Luke 24:19 KJV). In Greek, that's *"dunatos en ergoi."* The word for *deed*, in each case, comes from the same family.

Big deal.

That's what some defenders of the *Testimony* would say. The connections that some scholars have made to the gospel of Luke can read like quite the stretch—as though they come from folks desperate to believe that Jesus is a myth.

Defenders of the *Testimony* might add this: In the unlikely event that a Christian editor 1,700 years ago slipped into the *Testimony* a few words from the gospel of Luke, so what? Just about everyone already agrees that an editor tweaked the Greek version of Josephus's statement about Jesus—maybe even heavily edited it.

Josephus didn't write like this or use words like this. Bible and history experts have dissected the *Testimony* and performed what amounts to a literary biopsy. Instead of looking for malignant cells, they're looking for oddball words and phrases that don't match the writing of Josephus.

Take "the principal men among us," for example. That's a more literal translation of the "top Jewish leaders" who recommended the crucifixion of Jesus. Josephus refers to "principal men" dozens of times in his writing. But every time he connects the phrase to a specific location, and it's usually "principal men of Jerusalem" or "principal men of the city." Nowhere else, scholars note, does Josephus ever describe a group of leaders as "principal men among us."

On the other hand, who's to say "us" doesn't refer to the specific location where the people were standing at the time? In that case, Josephus may have been referring to Jerusalem or to the Jewish people as a scattered nation with no particular plot of ground they could call their own.

And another thing. Maybe Josephus never used the phrase like this before, but he did it now. Writers do deviate from the norm from time to time. Editors can confirm that.

Josephus skipped Nero's persecution of Christians. Why would Josephus mention Jesus and then skip Nero's devastating persecution of Jesus's followers? That's one of the questions some scholars ask.

The Great Fire of Rome burned much of the city in July of AD 64. Emperor Nero reportedly blamed the Christians and then began killing them in creative ways. He burned some on crosses in the arena, to entertain the crowds. Didn't work. The audience said it smelled bad.

Josephus was there in Rome for the better part of two years, beginning in AD 64. Yet he doesn't even mention Nero's vicious persecution.

There's an explanation, though.

Josephus said he wasn't going to report on anything about Nero. He didn't even mention the Great Fire. He said, "There have been a great many who wrote the history of Nero." He accused some writers of lying about the emperor: "They have no regard for the truth," he said, "They write whatever they want." As for Josephus, he said he would write nothing.

In fact, some scholars say Josephus had good reason to avoid any topics that could upset the politicians, since the Roman Empire provided him with a place to live and a pension. One of the main reasons he wrote anything at all was to help Romans better understand the Jewish people, their long tradition, and their faith. He put twenty volumes into that project, *Antiquities of the Jews*.

Josephus would have been harder on Jesus and the Christian movement. The Greek version of the *Testimony* praises a man that the Romans executed as a rebel king trying to boot the Romans out of the Jewish homeland. Writing about a man like that was no way for Josephus to endear himself and the Jewish people to the Roman Empire.

Some scholars say that even the neutral Syrian version is a problem. Though it stops short of excessively praising Jesus, it does compliment him as a wise man with a good reputation. If Josephus wanted to accurately report what the Jewish leaders said about Jesus, he would have trash-talked him as an enemy of both the Jewish people and the Roman Empire.

It sounds like some Christian editor got his hands on even this Syrian version of the *Testimony*. Many scholars agree. But they part company when some insist that Josephus had nothing at all to do with the *Testimony*. Other scholars argue that Josephus reported the core facts of the matter, while a Christian somewhere along the way may have inserted the kind words about Jesus.

WHY SOME PEOPLE ACCEPT JOSEPHUS'S JESUS

The* Testimony *dates to the beginning of the church. While critics complain that no one mentioned the Josephus quote for 300 years, defenders take the opposite approach. They say that at the very least, the *Testimony* goes all the way back to that point in history, when Eusebius became the first on record to mention it. That was in AD 324. Emperor

Constantine had decriminalized the Christian religion in AD 313, so Christianity had been legal for only about a decade. In the generation that followed, in AD 380, Christianity became the state religion of the Roman Empire.

Though Eusebius was the first on record to mention the *Testimony*, that doesn't mean he was the first to mention it. All it means is that of the documents uncovered so far, his is the earliest.

Josephus's second reference to Jesus points back to the first reference. Most historians agree that this is an authentic quote:

> . . . James, the brother of Jesus—the one who was called the Messiah. (*Antiquities of the Jews*, 20.9.1)

Like the earlier quote, this quote shows up in every copy of Josephus's *Antiquities of the Jews*.

Josephus reports that a newly appointed Jewish high priest, Ananus, convinced the 70-man Jewish supreme council known as the Sanhedrin to order James executed by stoning. The Bible writer who reported the story about how the church got started describes James as the leader of the Jerusalem church—which was the Mother Church of the Christian movement. There, at an emotionally charged church meeting, which included Peter and Paul, James was the last man talking after everyone else shut up (Acts 15).

Scholars say that Josephus's reference to Jesus here seems to point back to the earlier reference to Jesus in book 18. Josephus describes James as the brother of Jesus. But there were a lot of people called Jesus. It was a common name. It's the Greek version of Joshua, much like Esteban is the Spanish version of Stephen. To help identify which Jesus he was talking about, Josephus seems to refer to the Jesus he talked about earlier—"the one who was called the Messiah."

Messiah was a word worth avoiding. Clearly, Josephus thought so. The word conjured up bad memories of the Jewish rebels—Messiah wannabes—who launched failed revolts in attempts to drive out the Romans who were occupying the Jewish homeland. Josephus was writing the history of the Jews for his Roman hosts, to make the ancient Jewish faith more palatable for them, and more respectable. To do that, he needed to avoid talking about the longstanding Jewish habit of rebelling against any foreign force that tried to control them.

Josephus needed to avoid talking about why many Jewish scholars taught that God would send a warrior king from David's royal family to free them from Rome—a hope based on what their prophets had said.

> "The days are coming," declares the LORD,
>> "when I will raise up for David a righteous Branch,
> a King who will reign wisely
>> and do what is just and right in the land."
>>> (Jeremiah 23:5 NIV)

From the Roman point of view, that sounds like the seeds of insurrection. It would make Romans suspicious of the Jewish faith. So, Josephus avoided using the inflammatory word. He used it only to describe what some people thought of Jesus, who ended up crucified. That's what Romans call a happy ending.

Josephus was talking about THE Jesus. Almost all scholars agree that some Christian editor reworked the Greek version of *Testimony* of Josephus, to compliment Jesus and to make Josephus sound more Christian than Jewish. Tradition-minded scholars and progressives alike say they recognize that.

But many say they agree that if we gut the obvious Christianizing words, what's left is the heart of the message: Pilate ordered the crucifixion of Jesus.

This point of history tracks perfectly with the previous two stories Josephus told about Pilate. The story about Jesus is the third in a row of dumb decisions Pilate made.

Jesus is not the exception to the rule in this chapter, many argue.

Most scholars generally accept the reporting of Josephus as authentic, recognizing that he sometimes exaggerated about himself. They read his books and embrace the facts he reports.

So why should anyone make an exception for Jesus, and cut him out of the book as a late add-on? That's the question some ask of those who argue that Josephus never even mentioned Jesus.

GAIUS CORNELIUS TACITUS, in a drawing from an unknown artist in 1920. There's no known image of Tacitus.

CHAPTER 20

"THEY GOT THEIR NAME FROM CHRISTUS"

—TACITUS (AD 56–120)

*Roman senator and historian who tried
and executed Christians when he served as
a governor in what is now Turkey*

On the windy and sweltering night of July 18, AD 64, fire broke out in rundown shops around the Circus Maximus, Rome's huge stadium famous for chariot racing. The blaze erupted into a firestorm that raged for six days, flamed out, then reignited and burned another three days.

By then, two-thirds of Rome lay silent and charred—a city four times the size of New York's Central Park. Perhaps a million souls were suddenly homeless.

Several Roman writers, including a senator named Tacitus, reported that a rumor almost instantly emerged: Emperor Nero gave the order to set Rome on fire. As the rumor goes, he did it to gut poor sections of the city because he wanted to rebuild Rome into a jewel that would make him proud—which is what he later did. That's one reason some history scholars say Nero is a fair suspect.

Nero wanted to extinguish the nasty rumor. He outlined a strategy and started working his plan.

The next thing on the to-do list was to make peace with the gods. They consulted the Sibylline books [a collection of oracles, prophecies, and religious guidance].

Based on what the books said, they prayed to the gods Vulcan [god of fire], Ceres [goddess of crops], and Persephone [wife of Hades, god of the underworld]. . . .

Still, it made no difference what Nero did. It didn't matter how many lavish gifts the emperor donated. It didn't even matter what the gods did to restore the peace. Nothing could silence the rumors that the fire in Rome started because Nero gave the order.

To put those rumors to rest, Nero tied all the guilt and the

ROME BURNS. Christians took the heat for the fire that destroyed two-thirds of Rome. The blaze raged out of control for six days, and then another three when it reignited. Roman historian Tacitus said someone started a rumor that Nero ordered the fire. Nero, Tacitus reported, "Tied all the guilt and the worst possible punishment to a group of people hated for their disgusting behavior: Christians, they're called." That launched 300 years of on and off imperial persecution of Christians.

worst possible punishment to a group of people hated for their disgusting behavior: Christians, they're called.

They got their name from Christus, executed during the reign of Tiberius. One of our governors, procurator Pontius Pilate, sentenced him to death. That put an end to the superstition and its cult of troublemakers. Only temporarily, though.

Trouble broke out again. This time it wasn't just in Judea, where the superstition started. It spread all the way to Rome. No surprise since Rome is where everything miserable and despicable from all over the world eventually ends up—and becomes popular.

Officials arrested everyone who admitted to being a Christian. That turned into a massive crowd of criminals sentenced to die not so much for burning the city as for hating their fellow human beings.

Before executioners carried out the sentence, the crowds ridiculed Christians in every possible way. Then when it came time for them to die, executioners covered some in the skins of animals. Dogs tore those people apart. Others were nailed to crosses or burned alive as human torches to light the nighttime entertainment.

Annals, 15.44

CRITICS ENTER HERE

Most scholars say the words of Tacitus are authentic. He wrote them.

Yet there are some who push back against the idea that Tacitus was a witness confirming the life, death, and crucifixion of Jesus Christ.

They remind us that Tacitus

- never mentioned Jesus by name;

- messed up some facts that an official of his position should have gotten right; and

- repeated what Christians were saying at the time—so that what little he says about Christianity is merely hearsay.

Here's some of what students of history are debating about Tacitus:

OBJECTIONS	CRITICS	DEFENDERS
All we have are copies of the original book.	The oldest copy of *Annals* dates to the time of the Crusades, in about AD 1000. That's plenty of time for some well-meaning Christian editors to insert a little extra drama into the reporting. An "interpolation," scholars call it, or an "insertion."	Most historians today seem to accept the quote from Tacitus as authentic. It shows up in every known copy of *Annals*. It's written in Tacitus's unique style, which we could describe as Bad Latin. And the intense anti-Christian tone fits the attitude that he and other Roman leaders had toward Christians.
No mention by church leaders	During that first millennium, none of the early church leaders quoted this excerpt from Tacitus.	Early church leaders avoided quoting negative references to Jesus and to the Christian faith. They preferred to focus on the positive. They also may not have had access to what Tacitus wrote. He didn't write *Annals* for them; he wrote for the Romans.
Wrong title for Pilate	Tacitus got the title of Pilate wrong. He called him a procurator. Pilate was a military prefect, before Romans started shifting that title over to "procurator." So, Tacitus isn't reliable. (See photo on page 152.)	Big deal. Accidentally calling someone an Air Force pilot when he flew in 1941 and was actually an Army Air Corps pilot doesn't mean the dogfights never happened. Besides, Tacitus may have known the correct title but used the updated title, much like we know Corinth was in the Roman province of Achaia but we describe it to readers today as in southern Greece.
Wrong name of Jesus	Tacitus got the name of Jesus wrong. He identified Jesus by the title, *Christus*, which is the Latin word for the Hebrew term *Messiah—Anointed One* in English.	Even New Testament writers referred to Jesus by the title of Christ. And the name "Christ" allowed Tacitus to quickly link Jesus to the Christian movement since the names are obviously related.

OBJECTIONS	CRITICS	DEFENDERS
The passage is forged	There are too many factual errors. For one, "Christians" wasn't a common word at the time.	Christians were first known as the Way (Acts 19:23) but soon became known as Christians (Acts 11:26). Tacitus confirms that and adds that it was possible to distinguish between Christians and Jews. As for forgery, Josephus gets accused of it for saying kind things about Jesus, and now Tacitus gets accused of it for saying nasty things about Christianity. A Christian forger isn't likely to go nasty on his own faith.

LIGHT 'EM UP. On Emperor Nero's order, Christians tied to a post are about to provide evening light in the arena. Reports say he coated Christians in pine tar and wax and set them on fire.

PILATE WAS HERE. Someone with a chisel 2,000 years ago hammered Pontius Pilate's name into a limestone block, found in the seaside city of Caesarea. This is a replica of the stone at Caesarea; the original is in Jerusalem's Israel Museum. Rome used Caesarea as the capital of their province of Judea. That region is in what is now southern Israel and Palestinian Territory. The stone confirms the Bible's report that Pilate was governor of the Judean province. His job title was "prefect."

[*DIS AUGUST*]S TIBERIEUM

[*PONTI*]US PILATUS

[*PRAEF*]ECTUS JUDA[*EA*]

NOTABLE QUOTES FROM SCHOLARS NOTABLY CRITICAL

I don't know of any trained classicists or scholars of ancient Rome who think that the reference to Jesus in Tacitus is a forgery.

> Bart D. Ehrman, best-selling biblical scholar, who describes himself as an agnostic (*Did Jesus Exist?*, p. 55)

That [Jesus] was crucified is as sure as anything historical can ever be, since both Josephus and Tacitus . . . agree with the Christian accounts on at least that basic fact.

> John Dominic Crossan, New Testament scholar who sometimes stirs controversy in biblical circles with his critical approach to the Bible (*Jesus*, p. 45)

CHAPTER 21

THE CROSS: "A PERFECT ALTAR FOR THESE DEGENERATES"

—Marcus Minucius Felix

A century before the Roman Empire legalized Christianity in the mid AD 300s, a little-known writer named Marcus Minucius Felix (see page 107) wrote a book defending the outlawed Christian religion.

The book is *Octavius*, named after the starring character, a Christian lawyer, Octavius Januarius. Author Marcus Felix, in his book, attempts to correct warped and wild rumors about Christianity.

He does this in what reads like a fictional, first-person story that he narrates. It's a story about a polite argument he witnessed—and sometimes refereed. The story takes place on a holiday afternoon at an Italian beach in Ostia, a seaside town about a half-day's walk from Rome, roughly 10 miles (16 km). (See map page 111).

The topic of Christianity comes up when Marcus and his friend Octavius take a stroll along the beach with a non-Christian friend named Caecilius Natalis. Caecilius stops to pay his respects to a statue of Serapis, a god that some Romans and Egyptians said could heal the blind and overrule fate. Caecilius raises his hand to his mouth and pushes a kiss into his palm. Marcus described this as "the custom of the superstitious common folks."

Octavius politely condemns the worship of images carved into stone. Caecilius pushes back with his own thoughts about Christianity.

As wickedness and bad manners spread like weeds, so are those horrible Christian gatherings; they're cropping up all over the world. These are people who need to be hunted down and exterminated. . . .

Lust is all over this religion. These people call each other brothers and sisters. Then they invoke their religion's most sacred name [Jesus] as an excuse to practice incest. Their worthless superstition glorifies criminal behavior. . . .

I don't know if the accusations against them are true. But there's certainly good reason for suspicion.

For one: their secret, nighttime rituals.

For another: when they try to explain the reason for their rituals, they end up talking about a man executed for crimes so vile that he was hung on a wooden cross.

That makes the cross a perfect altar for these degenerates. Let them worship there. They deserve it.

Octavius, chapter 9

WORSHIPING A CRIMINAL. "Their worthless superstition glorifies criminal behavior. . . . When they try to explain the reason for their rituals, they end up talking about a man executed for crimes so vile that he was hung on a wooden cross. That makes the cross a perfect altar for these degenerates. Let them worship there. They deserve it." —Caecilius, in *Octavius*.

PART 3

WHAT THE BIBLE SAYS ABOUT JESUS'S CRUCIFIXION

CRUCIFIED JESUS. In Jerusalem, crowded with pilgrims who had come to celebrate the Jewish holiday of Passover, Romans crucify Jesus and two insurgents outside the city walls.

CHAPTER 22

FROM THE TRIAL TO THE CROSS TO THE GRAVE

You might be surprised what the gospel writers didn't say about the crucifixion of Jesus.

Some scholars say the gospel writers who told the story of Jesus didn't say that Jesus

- carried a T-shaped cross;

- carried a crossbeam;

- fell while carrying whatever part of the execution device he was carrying;

- was hung on a T-shaped cross; or

- was nailed to anything.

Christians merely presume this, those scholars say. People presume it by reading between the lines, adding educated guesses, and by accepting as fact the description of crucifixions that church leaders wrote a century or more later.

When Christians run the story of Jesus's crucifixion inside their head, it often plays like a familiar and cherished movie. They see Jesus carrying his cross, collapsing under its weight after his beating. They see Romans nailing him—hand and hand and feet—to a T-shaped cross.

But some Christian scholars are urging that we all should take a deep breath and carefully reconsider what the Bible writers actually did and didn't say about the execution of Jesus. It won't change the fact that Jesus died and rose again. Bible writers clearly said that happened. But it could change the way we picture how Jesus died.

The Greek word that all four gospel writers used to describe the instrument of execution is *stauros*. Scholars working on Bible versions translate the word into English as a "cross." But Greek writers like Homer used the same word to describe a pole or a fencepost. (See "Crucifixion dictionary," page 22).

That said, most Bible scholars seem to teach that there's good reason to believe Jesus died very much like most of us picture it: nailed to a T-shaped cross.

Some presumptions seem logical.

Yes, we can admit the Bible doesn't say Jesus fell under the weight of the cross or the crossbeam as he carried it to the execution site. But it does say the Romans conscripted Simon from Cyrene to carry the beam—or whatever it was. Why do that unless Jesus had fallen,

FIRST PAINTING OF JESUS ON CROSS. Jesus hangs nailed on the cross, in a painting from 1,500 years ago—just a couple hundred years after the Roman Empire legalized Christianity. It's the oldest-known painting of him crucified, and it's part of an illustrated Bible—a collection of the gospels about Jesus. The book is from the Syrian monastery of St. John of Zagba.

unable to carry the wood any further (Matthew 27:32; Mark 15:21; Luke 23:26)?

It's not as though a Roman soldier is going to say, "Hey, Jesus, King of the Jews, you're looking a little winded. Let me get you some help carrying that hunk of a tree, or pole, or whatever you want to call it."

Presumptions that fill in the details for us were reported as facts in the writings of early Christians during the first few generations after Jesus. Presumably they weren't presuming, but were reporting what eyewitnesses had seen and heard, and had passed along in unforgettable detail.

However, that's another presumption.

But there's more than presumption and Christian tradition behind the story of Jesus crucified and nailed to a cross, most Christian scholars seem to agree.

STRAIGHT OUT OF THE BIBLE

Gospel writers report the crucifixion of Jesus—covering it from his trial to his burial. Most of the details they report have parallels from history outside the Bible.

From trial to burial, here's what the Bible says about the crucifixion of Jesus. And where there's a parallel from Roman history outside the Bible, it's been included.

Roman trial

Matthew

"Leading priests and the elders of the people met again. . . . Then they bound him, led him away, and took him to Pilate, the Roman governor" (27:1–2).

Mark

"Leading priests, the elders, and the teachers of religious law—the entire high council—met to discuss their next step. They bound Jesus, led him away, and took him to Pilate, the Roman governor" (15:1).

Luke

"Then the entire council took Jesus to Pilate, the Roman governor" (23:1).

ON THE WAY TO THE CROSS. Roman governor Pilate interrogates Jesus.

John

"Jesus' trial before Caiaphas ended in the early hours of the morning. Then he was taken to the headquarters of the Roman governor" (18:28).

Writer outside the Bible

"Alexander, a slave of P. Atinius, was suspected of murdering the Roman knight C. Flavius. Judges ordered him tortured six times. But throughout the torture he said he had nothing to do with the murder. He might as well have confessed. The judges sentenced him to the cross" (*Valerius Maximus*, Of Words and Deeds, 8.4.2).

Mocked

Matthew

"Some of the governor's soldiers took Jesus into their headquarters and called out the entire regiment. They stripped him and put a scarlet robe on him. They wove thorn branches into a crown and put it on his head, and they placed a reed stick in his right hand as a scepter. Then they knelt before him in mockery and taunted, 'Hail! King of the Jews!' And they spit on him and grabbed the stick and struck him on the head with it. When they were finally tired of mocking him, they took off the robe and put his own clothes on him again. Then they led him away to be crucified" (27:27–31).

Mark

"The soldiers took Jesus into the courtyard of the governor's headquarters (called the Praetorium) and called out the entire regiment. They dressed him in a purple robe, and they wove thorn branches into a crown and put it on his head. Then they saluted him and taunted, 'Hail! King of the Jews!' And they struck him on the head with a reed stick, spit on him, and dropped to their knees in mock worship. When they were finally tired of mocking him, they took off the purple robe and put his own clothes on him again. Then they led him away to be crucified" (15:16–20).

Luke

"Herod and his soldiers began mocking and ridiculing Jesus. Finally, they put a royal robe on him and sent him back to Pilate" (23:11).

John

"The soldiers wove a crown of thorns and put it on his head, and they put a purple robe on him. 'Hail! King of the Jews!' they mocked, as they slapped him across the face" (19:2–3).

Jesus is taken to the military HQ, where soldiers humiliate him and mock him as a fake king.

Writer outside the Bible

Nero executed Christians in the arena at Rome in AD 64, apparently after blaming them for starting the fire that destroyed much of the city.

"Before executioners carried out the sentence, the Christians were ridiculed in every possible way. Then when it came time for them to die, some were covered in the skins of animals and torn apart by dogs. Others were nailed to crosses or burned alive as human torches to light the nighttime entertainment" (Tacitus, *Annals*, 15.44).

Beaten

Matthew

"Pilate released Barabbas to them. He ordered Jesus flogged with a lead-tipped whip, then turned him over to the Roman soldiers to be crucified" (27:26).

Mark

"To pacify the crowd, Pilate released Barabbas to them. He ordered Jesus flogged with a lead-tipped whip, then turned him over to the Roman soldiers to be crucified" (15:15).

Luke

"Pilate called together the leading priests and other religious leaders, along with the people, and he announced his

Roman soldiers beat Jesus, on orders from Roman governor Pontius Pilate.

verdict. . . . 'I will have him flogged, and then I will release him'"
(23:13–14, 16).

Writer outside the Bible

"There was this one time at the arena when a man dragged his slave out
in front of everyone. The games honoring the great god Jupiter hadn't
even started yet. But he took the slave out into the center of the circus.
The slave deserved severe punishment, and he got it. His master beat him
with rods. After that, he got the punishment that's customary for slaves:
the cross" (Arnobius of Sicca, *The Case Against the Pagans*, 2.7.39).

Carried the cross

Matthew

"They led him away to be crucified. Along the way, they came across a
man named Simon, who was from Cyrene, and the soldiers forced him
to carry Jesus' cross" (27:31–32).

Mark

"Then they led him away to be crucified. A passerby named Simon,
who was from Cyrene, was coming in from the countryside just then,
and the soldiers forced him to carry Jesus' cross" (15:20–21).

Luke

"As they led Jesus away, a man named Simon, who was from Cyrene,
happened to be coming in from the countryside. The soldiers seized
him and put the cross on him and made him carry it behind Jesus"
(23:26).

John

"So they took Jesus away. Carrying the cross by himself, he went to the
place called Place of the Skull" (19:16–17).

Writer outside the Bible

"The [sixteen] men were paraded out, chained together by the foot and
neck, each carrying his own cross. The executioners added this grim
public spectacle to the punishment as an extra deterrent to any slaves

Jesus falls under the weight of the cross, a detail the gospel writers never reported. That scene is assumed, since soldiers recruited a bystander, Simon of Cyrene, to finish carrying it for him. The word for "cross" might mean the cross, the crossbar, or just a pole.

thinking about committing the same crime" (Chariton, *Chaereas and Callirhoe*, 4.2).

Attached to the cross

Gospel writers describing the Crucifixion didn't say how Jesus was attached to the cross.

Many presume Romans nailed him to the cross. They presume it for various reasons. For one, the doubting disciple, Thomas, seemed to presume it. After he heard the news of the resurrection, he said, "I won't believe it unless I see the nail wounds in his hands" (John 20:25). Jesus appeared later, offering to show Thomas his injured hands and a wound in his side.

Luke says that the resurrected Jesus told his shocked disciples to "Look at my hands. Look at my feet" (Luke 24:39). That suggests he was showing his crucifixion wounds. Or could he have been saying something comparable to "Look at me from head to toe. It's really me, guys"?

Like Thomas, Paul seemed to assume Romans nailed Jesus to the cross. He wrote to the church in Colossae, a city in what is now Turkey, "God wiped out the charges that were against us for disobeying the Law of Moses. He took them away and nailed them to the cross" (Colossians 2:14 CEV).

Then there are the prophecies suggesting someone would drive nails into the Messiah: "He was pierced through for our transgressions" (Isaiah 53:5 NASB). "Dogs have surrounded me; A band of evildoers has encompassed me; They pierced my hands and my feet" (Psalm 22:16 NASB).

On the other hand, some Bible versions replace "pierced" with other words describing injury—such as "tearing at my hands and my feet" (Psalm 22:16 CEV).

Some Bible translations have the gospel writers describing the Crucifixion by saying Jesus was nailed to the cross. But more literal translations simply say he was crucified. No mention of nails.

Matthew

"They had crucified him" (27:35 NASB).

Soldiers nail Jesus to the cross, a detail that gospel writers don't confirm. The nails are presumed, partly from something the disciple Thomas said when he heard Jesus rose from the dead: "I will not believe it until I see the nail marks in his hands" (John 20:25 NCV).

Mark

"They crucified him" (15:24 NASB).

Luke

"When they came to the place called The Skull, there they crucified Him" (23:33 NASB).

John

"There they crucified Him" (19:18 NASB).

Writer outside the Bible

"Go nail yourself to a cross." (Graffiti in the public baths at Pompeii, an ancient Italian city destroyed by the eruption of Mount Vesuvius in AD 79.)

Scholars say the phrase was probably intended as profane or obscene, comparable to today's "Go to—."

Drink

It's unclear if the soldiers offered Jesus drinks as a painkiller or as just another taunt and torture.

Matthew

"The soldiers gave Jesus wine mixed with bitter gall, but when he had tasted it, he refused to drink it" (27:34).

"Some of the bystanders misunderstood and thought he was calling for the prophet Elijah. One of them ran and filled a sponge with sour wine, holding it up to him on a reed stick so he could drink. But the rest said, 'Wait! Let's see whether Elijah comes to save him'" (27:47–49).

Mark

"They offered him wine drugged with myrrh, but he refused it" (15:23).

Luke

"The soldiers mocked him, too, by offering him a drink of sour wine" (23:36).

John

"Jesus . . . said, 'I am thirsty.' A jar of sour wine was sitting there, so they soaked a sponge in it, put it on a hyssop branch, and held it up to his lips. When Jesus had tasted it, he said, 'It is finished!' Then he bowed his head and gave up his spirit" (19:28–30).

Writer outside the Bible

It doesn't seem that writers in Roman times reported any attempts to ease the pain of a crucified person. There are, however, examples of the opposite. Executioners tried to extend the victim's life to increase the pain.

A soldier offers Jesus a drink from a sponge dipped in sour wine.

"The crucified are hung above the ground on a wooden cross. They are nailed there, hands and feet, executed in a lingering death. In fact, people weren't crucified because someone merely wanted to kill them. People lived a long time on the cross—and not because they wanted to. Executioners prolonged the death because that prolonged the pain" (Augustine, *Tractate 36*).

Here's a note about a Chinese man crucified on Wednesday, October 28, 1863. Authorities charged him with kidnapping young girls and selling them as fresh-meat prostitutes. He was still alive on Saturday. A foreigner appealed to the top local official, called the Taotai, to put the man out of his misery.

"The Taotai . . . immediately gave orders that vinegar should be administered, which he expected would produce immediate death; but the result was otherwise, and at sunset . . . two soldiers with stout bamboos broke both his legs and then strangled him" (J. Jones, *On Punishment of Crucifixion in China*).

Guarded

Matthew

"Soldiers . . . sat around and kept guard as he hung there" (27:35–36).

Mark

"The Roman officer who stood facing him saw how he had died" (15:39).

Luke

"The Roman officer overseeing the execution saw what had happened" (23:47).

Writer outside the Bible

"The governor sentenced some robbers to be attached to crosses. . . .

That night, a soldier stood guard by the crosses to make sure no one pulled a corpse off and buried it" (Phaedrus, "Widow of Ephesus," *Satyricon of Petronius Arbiter*).

Sign announcing crime

Matthew

"A sign was fastened above Jesus' head, announcing the charge against him. It

Soldiers kept guard over Jesus and the other men crucified, to make sure no one took them off the cross.

read: 'This is Jesus, the King of the Jews'" (27:37).

Mark

"A sign announced the charge against him. It read, 'The King of the Jews'" (15:26).

Luke

"A sign was fastened above him with these words: 'This is the King of the Jews'" (23:38).

John

"Pilate posted a sign on the cross that read, 'Jesus of Nazareth, the King of the Jews.' The place where Jesus was crucified was near the city, and the sign was written in Hebrew, Latin, and Greek, so that many people could read it" (19:19–20).

A sign hangs above Jesus, announcing his crime of insurrection, as someone who claimed to be king of the Jews.

Writer outside the Bible

"Last of all comes the sign [called a *titulus*], which describes the reason for the punishment" (Quintilian, *The Lesser Declamations*, 380.2).

Crucified with others

Matthew

"Two revolutionaries were crucified with him, one on his right and one on his left" (27:38).

Mark

"Two revolutionaries were crucified with him, one on his right and one on his left" (15:27).

Luke

"Two others, both criminals, were led out to be executed with him" (23:32).

John

"Two others were crucified with him, one on either side, with Jesus between them" (19:18).

Writer outside the Bible

"A spy from Carthage had managed to avoid capture for two years, but he was eventually caught in Rome, with the help of an informer. The Romans cut off the spy's hands and set him free. But they crucified twenty-five of his slaves, charging them with the crime of conspiracy. The slaves were crucified at the Campus Martius. The informer was set free and rewarded with 20,000 sesterces [about 13 years of salary for

Jesus hangs between two convicted revolutionaries, which some would see as appropriate company for a man claiming to be a king.

a typical worker]" (Livy, *History of Rome*, 22.33.1–2).

Possessions taken

Matthew

"After they had nailed him to the cross, the soldiers gambled for his clothes by throwing dice" (27:35).

Mark

"Soldiers . . . divided his clothes and threw dice to decide who would get each piece" (15:24).

Luke

"Soldiers gambled for his clothes by throwing dice" (23:34).

Soldiers strip Jesus of his robe and gamble to see who gets the perk.

John

"When the soldiers had crucified Jesus, they divided his clothes among the four of them. They also took his robe, but it was seamless, woven in one piece from top to bottom. So they said, 'Rather than tearing it apart, let's throw dice for it.' This fulfilled the Scripture that says, 'They divided my garments among themselves and threw dice for my clothing.' So that is what they did" (19:23–24).

Writers outside the Bible

A crucifixion warning engraved in stone during the AD 200s, at the Greek town of Thessalonica: "Anyone caught opening any of these tombs or burying someone else in them risks death on a cross. All property belonging to that person will be confiscated and turned over to the city treasury."

"King Darius ordered that if anyone disobeys any of his written or spoken laws, or treats the laws as invalid, a beam of timber should be pulled from his house and he should be crucified [or impaled] onto it.

Everything that person owns will be confiscated and given to the king" (*1 Esdras 6:32*; this book appears in some Bibles, including those of Eastern Orthodox Christians).

Insulted, abused on the cross

Matthew

"The leading priests, the teachers of religious law, and the elders also mocked Jesus. 'He saved others,' they scoffed, 'but he can't save himself! So he is the King of Israel, is he? Let him come down from the cross right now, and we will believe in him! He trusted God, so let God rescue him now if he wants him! For he said, "I am the Son of God."' Even the revolutionaries who were crucified with him ridiculed him in the same way" (27:41–44).

Mark

"The people passing by shouted abuse, shaking their heads in mockery. 'Ha! Look at you now!' they yelled at him. 'You said you were going to destroy the Temple and rebuild it in three days. Well then, save yourself and come down from the cross!' The leading priests and teachers of religious law also mocked Jesus. 'He saved others,' they scoffed, 'but he can't save himself! Let this Messiah, this King of Israel, come down from the cross so we can see it

Jewish leaders ridicule Jesus as he hangs on the cross, dying.

and believe him!' Even the men who were crucified with Jesus ridiculed him. . . . One of [the bystanders] ran and filled a sponge with sour wine, holding it up to him on a reed stick so he could drink. 'Wait!' he said. 'Let's see whether Elijah comes to take him down!'" (15:29–32, 36).

Luke

"The crowd watched and the leaders scoffed. 'He saved others,' they said, 'let him save himself if he is really God's Messiah, the Chosen One.' The soldiers mocked him, too, by offering him a drink of sour wine. They called out to him, 'If you are the King of the Jews, save yourself!'" (23:35–37).

Writers outside the Bible

"First they [rebel Jews captured by Romans] were beaten. Then they were ridiculed. They were tortured in lots of different ways before they finally died, crucified outside Jerusalem's city walls" (Josephus, *War of the Jews* 5.11.1).

"When we crucify people, we do it on the busiest roads. We want as many people as possible to get a good look at it, and to feel the terror of it all. The punishment of crucifixion has relatively little to do with the crime. It's more about deterrence, and teaching people a lesson by example" (Quintilian, *Declamations* 274).

Death

Matthew

"At noon, darkness fell across the whole land until three o'clock. At about three o'clock, Jesus called out with a loud voice, '*Eli, Eli, lema sabachthani?*' which means 'My God, my God, why have you abandoned me?'. . . Then Jesus shouted out again, and he released his spirit. . . . The Roman officer and the other soldiers at the crucifixion were terrified by the earthquake and all that had happened. They said, 'This man truly was the Son of God!'" (27:45–46, 50, 54).

Mark

"At noon, darkness fell across the whole land until three o'clock. Then at three o'clock Jesus called out with a loud voice, '*Eloi, Eloi, lema sabachthani?*' which means 'My God, my God, why have you abandoned me? . . . Then

The sun falls dark at noon, earthquakes shake the ground, and Jesus dies. Even the soldiers now seem to recognize that there was something godlike about this man.

Jesus uttered another loud cry and breathed his last. And the curtain in the sanctuary of the Temple was torn in two, from top to bottom. When the Roman officer who stood facing him saw how he had died, he exclaimed, 'This man truly was the Son of God!'" (15:33–34, 37–39).

Luke

"It was about noon, and darkness fell across the whole land until three o'clock. The light from the sun was gone. And suddenly, the curtain in the sanctuary of the Temple was torn down the middle. Then Jesus shouted, 'Father, I entrust my spirit into your hands!' And with those words he breathed his last. When the Roman officer overseeing the execution saw what had happened, he worshiped God and said, 'Surely this man was innocent'" (23:44–47).

John

"Jesus . . . said, 'It is finished!' Then he bowed his head and gave up his spirit. It was the day of preparation, and the Jewish leaders didn't want the bodies hanging there the next day, which was the Sabbath. . . . So they asked Pilate to hasten their deaths by ordering that their legs be broken. Then their bodies could be taken down. So the soldiers came and broke the legs of the two men crucified with Jesus. But when they came to Jesus, they saw that he was already dead, so they didn't break his legs" (John 19:30–33).

Writer outside the Bible

"Your honors, I want to make sure you know that Verres erected the cross at a spot never before used for this in all of Messana's history. He picked the location because of what it allowed Gavius to see as he hung there, slowly dying in torture and agony. Gavius had a scenic view of Italy, just across the narrow strait. He could see the land of his liberty from the land that had enslaved him.

"Italy, too, could watch the murder of her son, killed in a manner so miserable and excruciating that it's fit for no one but slaves" (Cicero, *Against Verres*, 5.61–66).

Broken legs

John

"The soldiers came and broke the legs of the two men crucified with Jesus. But when they came to Jesus, they saw that he was already dead, so they didn't break his legs" (19:32–33).

Writer outside the Bible

"Hanno [leader of slaves attacking Carthage, about 360 BC] was captured in the process of encouraging Africans and the king of the Moors [in North Africa] to join his rebellion. First

With Jesus already dead, Roman soldiers break the legs of the other two crucified men so they'll die more quickly, possibly because they'd have to push up with their legs to catch a full breath.

of all, his captors clubbed him with rods. Then they tore out his eyeballs. Then they broke his arms and legs. It was as though they wanted to make sure every limb got its share of the punishment. Then finally, the public execution. They nailed his sliced and mangled body to a cross" (Paulus Orosius, *History Against the Pagans*, 4.6.19–20).

Stabbed by a spear

John

"When the soldiers came to Jesus and saw that he was already dead, they did not break his legs. But one of the soldiers stuck his spear into

Jesus' side, and at once blood and water came out. (The one who saw this happen is the one who told us this, and whatever he says is true. And he knows that he tells the truth, and he tells it so that you might believe)" (19:33–35 NCV).

A soldier confirms that Jesus is dead by stabbing him with a spear.

Writers outside the Bible

"The executioner will allow the burial of a crucified person who has been stabbed [to finish killing the victim]" (Quintilian, *Major Declamation* 6.9).

"Pilate didn't order anyone to stab Jesus under the arms even though Romans occasionally did that for people found guilty of serious crimes. Pilate didn't do it because he was afraid of the hostile energy in the crowd. But if people nailed to the cross weren't stabbed, they suffered in agony. It could go on all night long and clear through the next day" (Origen, *Commentary on Matthew*).

Burial

Matthew

"As evening approached, Joseph, a rich man from Arimathea who had become a follower of Jesus, went to Pilate and asked for Jesus' body. And Pilate issued an order to release it to him. Joseph took the body and wrapped it in a long sheet of clean linen cloth. He placed it in his own new tomb, which had been carved out of the rock. Then he rolled a great stone across the entrance and left. Both Mary Magdalene and the other Mary were sitting across from the tomb and watching" (27:57–61).

Mark

"This all happened on Friday, the day of preparation, the day before the Sabbath. As evening approached, Joseph of Arimathea took a risk and went to Pilate and asked for Jesus' body. (Joseph was an honored member of the high council, and he was waiting for the Kingdom of God to come.) Pilate couldn't believe that Jesus was already dead, so he called for the Roman officer and asked if he had died yet. The officer confirmed that Jesus was dead, so Pilate told Joseph he could have the body. Joseph bought a long sheet of linen cloth. Then he took Jesus' body down from the cross, wrapped it in the cloth, and laid it in a tomb that had been carved out of the rock. Then he rolled a stone in front of the entrance. Mary Magdalene and Mary the mother of Joseph saw where Jesus' body was laid" (15:42–47).

Luke

"Now there was a good and righteous man named Joseph. He was a member of the Jewish high council, but he had not agreed with the decision and actions of the other religious leaders. He was from the town of Arimathea in Judea, and he was waiting for the Kingdom of God to come. He went to Pilate and asked for Jesus' body. Then he took the body down from the cross and wrapped it in a long sheet of linen cloth and laid it in a new tomb that had been carved out of rock. This was done late on Friday afternoon, the day of preparation, as the Sabbath was about to begin. As his body was taken away, the women from Galilee followed and saw the tomb where his body was placed. Then they went

Followers of Jesus carry his body to a nearby tomb.

home and prepared spices and ointments to anoint his body. But by the time they were finished the Sabbath had begun, so they rested as required by the law" (23:50–56).

John

"Afterward Joseph of Arimathea, who had been a secret disciple of Jesus (because he feared the Jewish leaders), asked Pilate for permission to take down Jesus' body. When Pilate gave permission, Joseph came and took the body away. With him came Nicodemus, the man who had come to Jesus at night. He brought about seventy-five pounds of perfumed ointment made from myrrh and aloes. Following Jewish burial custom, they wrapped Jesus' body with the spices in long sheets of linen cloth. The place of crucifixion was near a garden, where there was a new tomb, never used before. And so, because it was the day of preparation for the Jewish Passover and since the tomb was close at hand, they laid Jesus there" (19:38–42).

Writer outside the Bible

"Romans had so little respect for people crucified that they simply threw out the corpses. No burial. Jews, however, are so careful to follow their own laws about burial rites that they will secretly take a body off the cross and bury it before sunset" (Josephus, *War of the Jews*, 4.317).

CHAPTER 23

WHEN CHRISTIANS STARTED TEACHING THAT JESUS DIED ON A CROSS

So, if the Bible doesn't clearly say Jesus died nailed onto a T-shaped cross, why do Christians put him there, with nails?

That's a fair question, asked by students of history who know that the word Bible writers used to describe the cross—*stauros*—meant "pole" in Greek literature. Many Roman writers may have used the word that way, too.

Here's the short answer.

Try to find an ancient picture of Jesus hanging on a pole.

Look for it in visual art such as drawings. Look for it in word pictures that clearly describe the instrument of Jesus's execution, which is something the Bible writers didn't do—and possibly didn't feel was necessary.

No luck?

Now look for some of the oldest pictures of crucifixion in Roman times—both in visual art and in words.

Here's some of what we find:

THE CROSS IN 2,000-YEAR-OLD VISUAL ART

Crucified jackass

Scratched into plaster on a wall in Rome within about 200 years of Jesus—and possibly during his century—there's a picture of a crucified person with a donkey head. The victim hangs from a T-shaped cross. It's called the Alexamenos ["Alexander" to us] graffito because the inscription seems to say "Alexamenos worships god."

There's no mention of Jesus or of Christians.

But there's what might be a relevant line from a book written in the early AD 200s that offers a link to Christianity. The book is by a Roman lawyer named Minucius Felix. He wrote a fictional conversation between a Christian and a non-Christian, in defense of Christianity. The two men were talking about Christianity when the non-Christian says this:

"I hear they revere the head of an ass, the lowest creature on earth" (*Octavius of Minucius Felix*, chapter 9).

DONKEY-HEADED JESUS? "Alexamenos worships god." That's the caption of a 2,000-year-old picture etched onto a wall in what was a Rome boarding school for messenger boys. Scholars say the picture and words are probably a dig at crucified Jesus and the Christians who worshiped him. The picture likely was drawn as early as Jesus's century or as late as the AD 200s. Romans spread rumors that Christians revered donkeys, much like some Hindus honor cows. A Christian named Tertullian, defending Christianity, wrote "Like some others, you've bought into the delusion that our god is an ass's head" (*Apology*, 16). This is a reproduction tracing, to make it easier to see the picture.

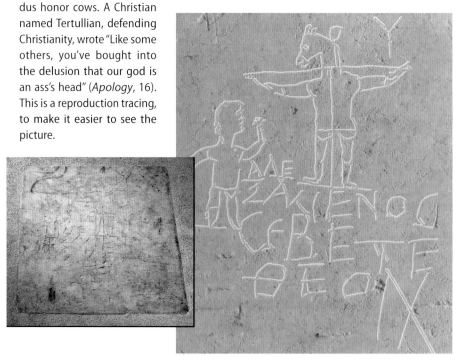

The words etched into the wall aren't a slam dunk. Experts in Roman history can't tell if Christianity is what the taunting artist had in mind when he defaced the wall. There are other theories. For example, the art might suggest that a Gnostic [secret-knowledge-based] religion that worshiped the ass-headed god Typhon-Seth merged with Christianity, which worshiped the crucified Christ.

Still, the donkey's head is also reminiscent of the donkey Jesus rode into Jerusalem one Sunday, while crowds cheered. By Friday morning, he was hanging on a cross, while crowds jeered.

Crucified with whipped back

It might take a scholar to see it, but some scholars say this, drawn on a hotel wall in the AD 100s, could be the picture of a crucified woman.

The graffito was discovered in 1959 in an ancient guest house for travelers at Puteoli, Italy. That's Pozzuoli today, south of Rome and near Naples. (See maps pages 47, 111.)

It seems impossible to tell if the picture is of a woman by looking at the picture alone, which is a few scribbles above a stick figure. But

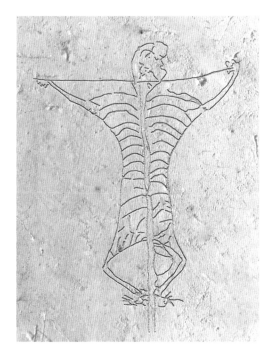

there's a faint inscription beside it—a woman's name, Alkimilla. Perhaps the artist was an eyewitness to crucifixions in the famous arena at Cumae, just a couple of miles (3 km) west, near the seacoast.

CRUCIFIED WITH STRIPES. A 2,000-year-old picture from a hotel wall near Naples and the famed arena at Cumae might show a crucified man with a lash-shredded back. Or it might show the back of a woman wearing a striped tunic. Scholars debate which. This is a replica, to make it easier to see the image.

The victim's arms stretch out on a crossbar. Her overlapping feet are anchored to the post perhaps by a nail. The artist doesn't seem to show ropes there, but did seem to go overboard with the length of the toes or the claw toenails.

The lash marks could be from a beating or a flaying—the painful torture of skinning a person alive. Some have suggested it's the woman's stripped tunic. But given what the Roman soldiers did with Jesus's robe—they gambled for it—some might wonder why anyone would nail a good tunic to a cross.

First-known picture of crucified Jesus

Perhaps the first surviving picture of Jesus in any form is the one of him engraved into a jasper gemstone an inch long (30 mm), and apparently once beveled into an oval to fit into someone's ring or necklace.

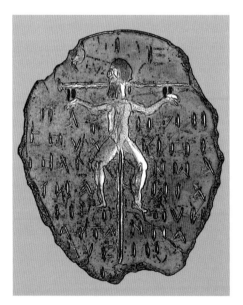

JESUS A GEM. Crucified Jesus, many scholars say, appears bearded and hanging tied to a cross. Someone engraved the image into a 2,000-year-old jasper gem once shaped into an oval, possibly for a ring or a necklace. The inscribed Greek words, which read like excerpts from prayers and songs, begin with "Oh Son, Father, Oh Jesus Christ." This is a reproduction, to make it easier to see the detail.

Scholars date the engraving to a few generations after Jesus, sometime in the late AD 100s or early 200s. That's when Christianity was still trying to figure out who Jesus was and how to understand the Trinity (which church fathers said they never did figure out, but they believed anyhow). It's also when Romans were still crucifying people, Christians included.

Words engraved in Greek begin with "Oh Son, Father, Oh Jesus Christ," according to some who have studied the text. Scholars say it sounds like an odd version of the Trinity: Son, Father, Jesus. No Spirit. What follows, they say, are words that sound like excerpts from Christian hymns, prayers, and statements of faith in the power of Jesus's crucifixion to save people—especially the person with this gemstone.

Some scholars speculate that the picture of Jesus was engraved by someone who didn't know the stories in the Gospels, since the picture doesn't show Jesus nailed in a way that would wound his hands and feet.

Instead, Jesus hangs tied to a crossbar with loose-hanging ropes. His feet dangle as though he's sitting on a block of wood that's nailed to the cross as a small seat, known in Rome's Latin as a *sedile*.

The back of the gemstone, apparently engraved later, includes ritual words and names used in magical incantations.

Jesus on the front. Magic on the back. Jasper in the middle.

The bases were loaded.

THE CROSS IN EARLIEST CHRISTIAN LITERATURE AFTER THE BIBLE

Early church fathers who began to write about their faith during the first centuries after Jesus, didn't put Jesus on a pole when they wrote about the Crucifixion. They described the Cross. Some say Jesus did, too.

Jesus

Some students of the Bible say they see a hint of Jesus's own cross in a warning he gave to Peter: "When you are old, you will stretch out your hands" (John 21:18). Peter was reportedly crucified upside down in Rome about 35 years later.

Anonymous author writing sometime between AD 70–130

Note: Hebrew and Greek letters of the alphabet had numerical equivalents

> The Bible says, "Abraham circumcised 18 men of his household and 300 others." What can we learn from this? We can see that he mentioned the 18 first. The 300 others came later. We get the first two letters of Jesus's name from 18. Ten is the numerical equivalent for 'I' and eight is the equivalent for 'H.' That's

Jesus [*Ihsous* in Greek, abbreviated IHC for "Jesus Christ"]. Then comes the 300, which is the numerical equivalent for the letter 'T.' Since the cross is T-shaped, we can see grace in all of this. Abraham showed us Jesus in two letters, and the cross in one.

> *Letter of Barnabas* 9:7, a document that some
> church leaders said belonged in the Bible. In fact,
> it's in the back of one of the oldest surviving Bibles:
> *Codex Sinaiticus*, copied in the AD 300s.

The argument that the *Letter of Barnabas* makes might seem convoluted today—and laughable. But scholars at the time taught that there were important meanings hidden in symbols and written between the lines of sacred books. Some taught that the symbolic meaning was as important as the obvious meaning. Sometimes more important, because God had hidden it from most people.

Justin Martyr (about AD 100–165)

Justin, a defender of Christianity in word and pen, was eventually beheaded, and so earned the rest of his name: Justin Martyr. He said the cross is everywhere.

> Prophet Isaiah, inspired by the Spirit, prophesied about Jesus Christ when he said, "I have spread out my hands to rebel-hearted people who deny the truth" [Isaiah 65:2]. . . .
>
> The prophet predicted what would become the Lord Christ's greatest symbol of both his role here and his power. Look around. We can see it everywhere. Think about everything in this world, and whether or not anything would work or could get done without objects formed into this shape. We couldn't travel the sea without a sail on the ship. We couldn't plow the ground. Workers couldn't fix broken things or dig wells or trenches without tools crafted into this shape. Humans differ from ignorant animals in nothing more obvious than our posture, as we stand erect with arms stretched out left and right. . . . All of these showcase no form but the cross.
>
> *First Apology*, chapters 35, 55

Irenaeus (AD 140–202), bishop in what is now France

> The cross has five distinct extremities. Two vertical [top and bottom]. Two horizontal [left and right]. One in the middle [a block of wood as small seat].
>
> *Against Heresies*, 2.24.4

Anonymous author writing from first century to the AD 200s

> I stretched my arms left and right, worshiping my Lord. I make his sign of the cross when I do this. For when I stand arms stretched out, I become the Cross.
>
> *Odes of Solomon*, 27

KEEP IT COMING KINDLY

As I write these last words in this last chapter of the book, that homemade video I did about Roman crucifixion has tallied about 1.7 million views and over 11,000 comments. I read every comment, including thousands that no one else reads; I have a filter that blocks comments laced in profanity and hateful words.

Some get through, often because of creative spelling or coded symbols

MARKS OF THE CROSS. The shape of the cross shows up even in people, when they stretch out their arms left and right. St. Francis of Assisi was famous for his wound marks on his hands and feet, called the *stigmata*, from the Greek word *stigma*, which means a tattoo mark. He is said to have received the marks during a vision.

that others recognize. Who knew that triple parentheses or brackets such as (((miller))) is an anti-Semitic way of calling me a Jew or a Jew-lover. I'm not Jewish, but I do try to be a people-lover. Some are more lovable than others—a single parentheses person, for example.

I reply to as many comments as I can, to those that seem reasonable. Some folks aren't interested in a conversation or an explanation.

If 11,000 comments can produce a fair sampling of what Christians and non-Christians think about the crucifixion of Jesus (and most scientific studies sample far fewer people than that), let me tell you which three criticisms have seemed most persistent and entrenched:

- Jesus never existed; he's a myth dreamed up by Bronze Age desert dwellers sitting bored around a campfire after a day of herding sheep.

- Neither Josephus nor Tacitus wrote anything about Jesus; Christians edited Jesus into those books.

- Jesus didn't die on a cross; he died on a pole. Some say a tree. I suggest a compromise: wood. Apparently, that's not good enough for those folks.

I've watched how Christians have responded to these and other criticisms, as they come to the defense of Jesus, or to their mental image of him hanging on the cross. Some Christians get verbally animated and even nasty.

I've had atheists write me to say that after reading the comments of Christians, they're glad they're not one of them—and that those of us who are Christians should be ashamed.

I am. Sometimes.

I don't want to be.

While Christians often hit the outsiders hard, they often do the same to me when I ask the wrong questions or present the other side of an argument.

Today, as I write this, a man who insisted that Jesus was nailed to the cross—not tied—sent me a link to an Old Testament prophecy about someone getting nailed, with pierced hands and feet. I reminded him that he was quoting Hebrew poetry and he was taking it literally, and presuming it referred to Jesus (which it may have, since New Testament writers presumed as much).

He insisted it's not poetry, but "accurate descriptions of the standard Roman crucifixion, as described in many historical documents."

Clearly he wasn't ready to hear that the prophecies were, in fact, written as Hebrew poetry. The words don't rhyme, but the lines do dance. The first line says one thing, and the second might say it again another way or might go in the opposite direction, as a contrast. That's how Hebrew poetry swings.

And he wasn't ready to hear that Romans didn't always work their way down a crucifixion checklist of standard operating procedures. I had already told him that Roman and Christian writers both said the Romans crucified people in different ways over the centuries.

So I told him I'd give him the last word.

He typed into the comment box: "Your petty mewlings about not 'assuming' are nothing more than pseudo-intellectual pretensions."

With that, he ended pretty much like he had started: "You should stop presuming to reject the plain testimony of God's Word on the subject. It looks very intellectual, I suppose, but it's not."

I had to look up "pseudo-intellectual."

In the discussions we have about Jesus with people both inside and outside the faith, I've come to believe we need to work harder at being kinder and more patient. I know I do. I'm getting better, I think. I was tempted to reply to the demeaning gentleman with a single, descriptive word that is not in the least bit intellectual. But I resisted.

Still, I wanted to. So, I guess I still have some work to do.

About the matter of how Jesus died, I suspect that most Christians have a detailed storyboard in their head, put there by Bible study, sermons, and movies.

As a result of this book, some Christians may reevaluate that picture and decide that it's okay if we don't have all the details. They'll conclude that we don't need to know if Jesus carried a T or a crossbar, and that it's not essential to know whether he was tied or nailed or both—and whether it was to a cross or a stake. Not likely a tree, since Simon of Cyrene was no Samson, as far as history reports.

How Jesus died is important. When someone we love dies, we naturally want to know how it happened. And with Jesus, even more so, because our spiritual salvation depends on what happened at this death and resurrection.

Yet how he died isn't as important as why he died.

Jesus told his disciples a few days before the Crucifixion: "If I am lifted up from the earth, I will draw all people toward me" (John 12:32 NCV).

Josephus said, "The disciples of Jesus didn't give up on him. They kept believing what he taught them" (*Antiquities of the Jews* 18.3.3). And they kept teaching what he taught them.

One of the biggest surprises to me about the simple, homemade crucifixion video I did, besides the fact that it caught some sort of viral wave and picked up a million views, is that it has somehow drawn thousands of atheists and agnostics into the conversation. I believe they have written more comments than the Christians.

WORDS OF A SKEPTIC

Here are excerpts of one exchange I had with a skeptic. It's posted in the YouTube comments with the crucifixion video, and remains a matter of public record.

Alex: What a wasted life you've had.

Steve: Have we met?

Alex: No, but I can tell.

Steve: That's called presumption. It's uninformed and unkind.

Alex: Actually, I've done what all great scientists do. I've looked at the evidence, from this video and others, and I've come to the conclusion that, unfortunately, you're just another duped sheep, following a book (the greatest lie ever told), which wasn't written at the time, or even by people of the time.

Steve: One of the core teachings of the Bible is to treat people kindly. From my point of view, to do otherwise is to waste the life we've been given.

Alex: But you must understand, that the bible only exists to you, in your world. And hey, I treat people just fine thanks, but I will point out stupidity, hence why you fell onto my radar.

Steve: There's more going on than the Bible. Here's a short video I did called 2 reasons I believe in God. [Shortly thereafter, that video got its first thumbs-down.] Badmouthing someone we've never met and know almost nothing about isn't something we generally associate with a scientist. We're more likely to expect it of an adolescent. . . .

Alex: Ok, that's a fair point. . . . I just find it so strange people hinge their whole lives because a book told them to. It honestly baffles me.

Steve: Christians read that book in widely different ways. Some . . . take it literally and say it is error-free. Others allow for humanity in the process: mistakes, copying errors, additions, deletions. There are things in there that most Christians reject: Paul telling women to keep quiet in church. No wonder he was a bachelor. For many Christians, the main takeaway is to treat people kindly, love God, and take care of the planet entrusted to our care. And the hope, of course, is that there is life in some fashion beyond this life. For many of us, there's a lot of "I don't know" in our faith. But we trust that this remarkable creation has a remarkable Creator. I know this is something scientists can't handle because they can't prove it. I have scientists in my family, so I get it. Still, given what I've lived and learned of life, there's something going on behind the scenes that we don't understand. I don't expect everyone to agree with me. But the people who know me well, scientists among them, know I'm no fool, but I do try to live the kind of life Jesus taught. And I am counting on Jesus to fulfill his promise of a life to come. If I'm wrong, I've lived a kind life and hopefully made my corner of the neighborhood a place where people knew they were considered important and loved. I'd be okay with that.

Alex: That is a fair answer, and one I respect. I guess my anger comes from street preachers, who publicly force their beliefs on others, and the religious people who judge the non-religious because of a book.

Did Jesus have people like Alex in mind when he said that if he is lifted up he will draw people to himself? Maybe he wasn't talking about his crucifixion. Maybe he was talking about getting lifted up in the resurrection or later in the ascension. But I can assure you that his crucifixion is still drawing people toward him and his teachings.

When it does, the cross opens a door for us. This gives us a chance to kindly say hello, welcome, and here's what I believe.

We might not harvest wheat that day. But we've planted seed.

Peace to you.

ART CREDITS

Page 8: 701 BC. Photo by Stephen M. Miller, British Museum.

Page 8: 73 BC. Painting by Fyodor Bronnikov, photo by *Wikimedia* (This work is in the public domain in its country of origin and other countries and areas where the copyright term is the author's life plus 100 years or fewer.)

Page 8: 44 BC. Photographer unknown, *Wikimedia.* (This work is in the public domain in its country of origin and other countries and areas where the copyright term is the author's life plus 100 years or fewer.)

Page 9: AD 30–33. Painting by Diego Velázquez (1599–1660), *Wikimedia.* (This work is in the public domain in its country of origin and other countries and areas where the copyright term is the author's life plus 100 years or fewer.)

Page 9: AD 46. Facial composite of Saint Paul, created by experts of the Landeskriminalamt of North Rhine-Westphalia using historical sources, proposed by Düsseldorf historian Michael Hesemann, *Wikimedia.*

Page 9: AD 64. Painting by Caravaggio (1571–1610), *Pixabay*

Page 9: AD 68. Painting by Vasily Smirnov. *Wikimedia.* (This work is in the public domain in its country of origin and other countries and areas where the copyright term is the author's life plus 100 years or fewer.)

Page 9: AD 70. Painting by Francesco Hayez, *Wikimedia.* (This work is in the public domain in its country of origin and other countries and areas where the copyright term is the author's life plus 100 years or fewer.)

Page 10: AD 79. Painting by Carlo Bonavia, photo from *Wikimedia*, public domain.

Page 10: AD 90. Photo by Olivierw, *Wikimedia*, enhanced by Stephen M. Miller. (This work is in the public domain in its country of origin and other countries and areas where the copyright term is the author's life plus 100 years or fewer.)

Page 10: AD 303. Photo by Stephen M. Miller, British Museum.

Page 10: AD 313. Photo by Jebulon, *Wikimedia* CC0 1.0. Original formerly at the Lateran Palace; gift of Sixtus IV, 1471.

Page 14: 206 BC. Photo by Sailko, *Wikimedia*, CC 3.0, creativecommons.org /licenses/by-sa/3.0/legalcode.

Page 14: 70 BC. Photo of bust by Carole Raddato, Capitoline Museums, *Wikimedia*, CC 2.0, creativecommons.org/licenses/by-sa/2.0/legalcode.

Page 14: 20 BC. Metropolitan Museum of Art, The Cesnola Collection, Purchased by subscription, 187476, *Wikimedia.*

Page 14: AD 40–45 Antikensammlung Berlin, *Wikimedia*, CC 3.0, creativecommons.org/licenses/by-sa/3.0/deed.en.

Page 37: Bag 'Em. Collage by Stephen M. Miller. Images by *Wikimedia*, CC 2.0, creativecommons.org/licenses/by-sa/2.0/deed.en . Dog: © Ad Meskens / Wikimedia Commons. Rooster: Amphipolis. Monkey: Cropped from a larger piece from Mary Gillham Archive Project. Man/background image: (This work is in the public domain in its country of origin and other countries and areas where the copyright term is the author's life plus 100 years or fewer.)

Page 39: Creative Hanging. Drawing by Lucas Cranach the Elder, *Wikimedia*. (This work is in the public domain in its country of origin and other countries and areas where the copyright term is the author's life plus 100 years or fewer.)

Page 42: Christian Martyrs' Last Prayer. This is detail from a larger painting by Jean Léon Gérôme, Walters Art Museum, *Wikimedia*. (This work is in the public domain in its country of origin and other countries and areas where the copyright term is the author's life plus 100 years or fewer.)

Page 44: Marcus Tullis Cicero. Photo of bust by Carole Raddato, Capitoline Museums, *Wikimedia*, CC 2.0, creativecommons.org/licenses/by-sa/2.0/legalcode.

Page 44: Rome Forum Ruins. Painting by Constantin Hansen (1804–1880), *Wikimedia*. (This work is in the public domain in its country of origin and other countries and areas where the copyright term is the author's life plus 100 years or fewer.)

Page 51: Nailed Ankle Bone. Stephen M. Miller.

Page 52: View to Die For. Photo by Shifegu, *Wikimedia*, CC 3.0, creativecommons.org/licenses/by/3.0/legalcode.

Page 53: Sky Burial. Photo by Chensiyuan, *Wikimedia*, CC 3.0, creativecommons.org/licenses/by-sa/3.0/legalcode.

Page 56: Quintus Horatius Flaccus. Metropolitan Museum of Art, The Cesnola Collection, Purchased by subscription, 1874–76, *Wikimedia*.

Page 57: Bird Watching. *Pixabay*.

Page 58: Burial Portrait. Painting from *Wikimedia*, no known copyright restrictions.

Page 60: Creative Crucifixion. Composite of public domain paintings by Antonello da Messina (1430–1479) of crucified men and James Tissot (1836–1902) "Reconstruction of Golgotha and the Holy Sepulchre, Seen from the Walls of Herod's Palace."

Page 61: Jerusalem Falls. Painting by Francesco Hayez, *Wikimedia*. (This work is in the public domain in its country of origin and other countries and areas where the copyright term is the author's life plus 100 years or fewer.)

Page 62: Titus. Photo © José Luiz Bernardes Ribeiro / CC BY-SA 4.0, *Wikimedia*, creativecommons.org/licenses/by-sa/4.0/.

Page 63: Vespasian. Photo by Alessandro Antonelli, *Wikimedia*, CC 3.0, creativecommons.org/licenses/by-sa/3.0/legalcode.

Page 66: Mass Execution. Art by Willem Swidde, color added to crucifixion field. (This work is in the public domain in its country of origin and other countries and areas where the copyright term is the author's life plus 100 years or fewer.)

Page 67: Antiochus IV Epiphanes. Photo by Classical Numismatic Group, Inc., http://www.cngcoins.com, *Wikimedia* CC 2.5, creativecommons.org /licenses/by-sa/2.5/legalcode.

Page 68: Crucified Women. Painting by Louis Joseph Raphaël Collin (1850–1916), *Wikimedia*. (This work is in the public domain in its country of origin and other countries and areas where the copyright term is the author's life plus 100 years or fewer.) Imaged edited by Stephen M. Miller, with apologies to the artist.

Page 69: Isis Priests Crucified. Photo by Miguel Hermoso Cuesta, *Wikimedia*, CC 3.0, creativecommons.org/licenses/by-sa/3.0/legalcode.

Page 71: Mosaic of Actors in Pompeii, Italy. © Ad Meskens / Wikimedia Commons, CC 3.0, creativecommons.org/licenses/by-sa/3.0/deed.en.

Page 73: What's Your Bid? "Slave Market in Ancient Rome" by Jean-Léon Gérôme (18241904), photo by Hermitage Torrent, *Wikimedia*. (This work is in the public domain in its country of origin and other countries and areas where the copyright term is the author's life plus 100 years or fewer.) A robe was added to the slave woman, to protect sensitive eyes, with apologies to Gérôme and art aficionados.

Page 76: Unknown Man from First Century. Photo by Sailko, *Wikimedia* CC 3.0, creativecommons.org/licenses/by/3.0/legalcode.

Page 78: Death Mold. Photo by Jebulon, *Wikimedia*, CC 1.0.

Page 79: Goodbye Pompeii. Map by Stephen M. Miller. Ships by Ji-Elle, *Wikimedia*, CC 3.0, and Deror avi, *Wikimedia* CC 3.0, creativecommons.org/licenses /by-sa/3.0/legalcode.

Page 80: Wounded Warrior. Photo by Wolfgang Rieger, *Wikimedia*. (This work is in the public domain in its country of origin and other countries and areas where the copyright term is the author's life plus 70 years or fewer.)

Page 81: Bad Dog. Photo by Walters Art Museum, *Wikimedia*, CC 3.0, creativecommons.org/licenses/by-sa/3.0/legalcode.

Page 82: Funeral Portrait of a Roman Man. Photo by Matthias Kabel, *Wikimedia*, CC 3.0, creativecommons.org/licenses/by-sa/3.0/legalcode.

Page 84: Witchcraft RX. Painting of Circe by Franz von Stuck (18631928), public domain; nails are a collection of Auckland Museum Tamak Paenga Hira, 2014.9.1, *Wikimedia*, CC 4.0, creativecommons.org/licenses/by/4.0/legalcode.

Page 86: Sketch of Plutarch. Digital art by Stephen M. Miller, from photo by Odysses, *Wikimedia*, CC 3.0, creativecommons.org/licenses/by-sa/3.0/legalcode.

Page 88: Cross of Sin. Painting by Biagio d'Antonio (1446–1516), photo by Brad Miller, Louvre. Used by permission.

Page 90: Crucified on a Ship's Mast. Digital image by Stephen M. Miller is based on part of a wall painting found in the ruins of King Herod's Herodian palace commemorating the Battle of Actium, *Wikimedia*, creativecommons.org/licenses

/by-sa/2.0/legalcode. Photo of quail by Yathin sk, Wikimedia, CC 3.0, creative commons.org/licenses/by-sa/3.0/legalcode.

Page 92: Chain Gang. Photo by Jun, *Wikimedia*, CC 2.0, creativecommons.org /licenses/by-sa/2.0/deed.en.

Page 95: Spartan Warrior. *Pixabay.*

Page 98: Funeral Portrait. Photo by Jon Bodsworth, *Wikimedia*, public domain.

Page 101: Cross, Front and Center. Photo by Brad Miller. Used by permission.

Page 103: Engraving of Eusebius. *Wikimedia*, public domain.

Page 105: Christians in the Bullseye. Photo by Jebulon, *Wikimedia*, public domain.

Page 106: Starving Upside Down. Painting by Caravaggio (1571–1610), *Pixabay.*

Page 108: The Cross Is Everywhere. Photo by Giorces, *Wikimedia*, CC 2.5, creativecommons.org/licenses/by/2.5/legalcode.

Page 109: Engraving of Livy. Photo from Rogers Fund, Metropolitan Museum of Art, *Wikimedia*, CC0 1.0.

Page 111: Hannibal, Lost with Elephants. Map by Stephen M. Miller.

Page 113: Lactantius. Photo by FA2010, *Wikimedia*, public domain.

Page 114: "Christians Can't Kill." Painting by James Tissot (1886–1902), Brooklyn Museum, *Wikimedia.*

Page 117: Last Man Standing. Painting by Jean-Léon Gérôme (1824–1904), photo by Phoenix Art Museum, *Wikimedia.* (This work is in the public domain in its country of origin and other countries and areas where the copyright term is the author's life plus 100 years or fewer.)

Page 119: Marcus Valerius Martialis. Sculpture by Juan Cruz Melero (1910–1986), photo by VICMAEL Victor Manuel, *Wikimedia.*

Page 121: Appian. Photo by shakko, *Wikimedia*, CC 3.0, creativecommons.org /licenses/by-sa/3.0/legalcode.

Page 122: Dead Army of Spartacus. Painting by Fyodor Bronnikov, photo by *Wikimedia* (This work is in the public domain in its country of origin and other countries and areas where the copyright term is the author's life plus 100 years or fewer.)

Page 124: Gaius Suetonius Tranquillus. Sketch based on photo by Frachet, *Wikimedia*, CC BY-SA 1.0.

Page 128: No Eyewitnesses on Record. Painting by Hendrick ter Brugghen, photo by Metropolitan Museum of Art, *Wikimedia.* (This work is in the public domain in its country of origin and other countries and areas where the copyright term is the author's life plus 100 years or fewer.)

Page 132: Bone Box for Brother of Jesus. Paradiso, *Wikimedia.* Photo was enhanced to show detail.

Page 134: Family Reunion. Sketch by Leonardo da Vinci (1452–1519), photo by National Gallery, *Wikimedia*. (This work is in the public domain in its country of origin and other countries and areas where the copyright term is the author's life plus 100 years or fewer.)

Page 146: Gaius Cornelius Tacitus. Adapted from *The Book of History: A History of All Nations from the Earliest Times to the Present*, vol. 7: The Roman Empire (New York: Grolier Society, 1920), p. 2741, *Wikimedia*. (The work is in the public domain in the United States because it was published [or registered in the U.S. Copyright Office] before January 1, 1924.)

Page 148: Rome Burns. Painting by Robert Hubert (1733–1808), *Wikimedia*. (This work is in the public domain in its country of origin and other countries and areas where the copyright term is the author's life plus 100 years or fewer.) Color edited by Stephen M. Miller.

Page 151: Light 'Em Up. Painting by Henryk Siemiradzki (1843–1902), *Wikimedia*. (This work is in the public domain in its country of origin and other countries and areas where the copyright term is the author's life plus 100 years or fewer.) Color edited.

Page 152: Pilate Was Here. Photo by Stephen M. Miller.

Page 154: Worshiping a Criminal. Painting by Diego Velázquez (1599–1660), *Wikimedia*. (This work is in the public domain in its country of origin and other countries and areas where the copyright term is the author's life plus 100 years or fewer.)

Page 156: Crucified Jesus. "A Crucifixion in the Time of the Romans" by Vasily Vereshchagin (1842–1904), Photo by Christie's, *Wikimedia*. (This work is in the public domain in its country of origin and other countries and areas where the copyright term is the author's life plus 100 years or fewer.)

Page 158: First Painting of Jesus on Cross. The Yorck Project, *Wikimedia*, public domain worldwide.

Page 160–178: On the Way to the Cross. Various paintings from the life of Christ by James Tissot (1836–1902), Brooklyn Museum, *Wikimedia*. (These works are in the public domain in their country of origin and other countries and areas where the copyright term is the author's life plus 100 years or fewer.)

Page 180: Donkey-Headed Jesus? Reproduction tracing by Stephen M. Miller; inset photo by Comrad King, *flickr*, CC 1.0.

Page 181: Crucified with Stripes. Replica by Stephen M. Miller.

Page 182: Jesus a Gem. Reproduction tracing by Stephen M. Miller.

Page 185: Marks of the Cross. "St Francis of Assisi adoring the Crucifix" by Bernardo Strozzi (1581–1644), *Wikimedia*, (This work is in the public domain in its country of origin and other countries and areas where the copyright term is the author's life plus 100 years or fewer.)

TOPICAL INDEX

Quotations are indicated in **bold**.
Illustrations are indicated in red.

ABOUT THE AUTHOR

Stephen M. Miller is an award-winning, best-selling author. He's a seminary-educated former news journalist who writes easy-reading books about the Bible and Christianity. *The Complete Guide to the Bible* has sold over 600,000 copies. *Who's Who and Where's Where in the Bible* won the Retailer's Choice Award as best nonfiction book of the year. *The Bible: A History* won best nonfiction book of the year in England. He lives in Kansas with his wife. They have two grown children, four grandchildren, and five dogs among the three families.

Websites:
StephenMillerBooks.com
CasualEnglishBible.com

Email address:
Steve@StephenMillerBooks.com

YouTube:
https://www.youtube.com/user/StephenMillerBooks

Vimeo:
https://vimeo.com/stephenmmiller

Facebook:
https://www.facebook.com/StephenMillerAuthor/

Twitter:
https://twitter.com/StephenMMiller_

Help us get the word out!

Our Daily Bread Publishing exists to feed the soul with the Word of God.

If you appreciated this book, please let others know.

- Pick up another copy to give as a gift.
- Share a link to the book or mention it on social media.
- Write a review on your blog, on a bookseller's website, or at our own site (ourdailybreadpublishing.org).
- Recommend this book for your church, book club, or small group.

Connect with us:

 @ourdailybread

 @ourdailybread

 @ourdailybread

Our Daily Bread Publishing
PO Box 3566
Grand Rapids, Michigan 49501 USA

 books@odb.org